ISRAEL

An Illustrated History

ISRAEL

An Illustrated History

David C. Gross

HIPPOCRENE BOOKS, INC.
New York

ISBN 0-7818-0756-5

For information, address:
HIPPOCRENE BOOKS, INC.
171 Madison Avenue
New York, NY 10016

Printed in the United States of America.

DEDICATION

To my maternal great-grandparents who, in the final years of the nineteenth century, departed Czarist Russia with its never-ending pogroms, to spend their final days in the Holy Land and to be interred in its sacred soil.

Little did they know that in the century following their demise, many hundreds of thousands of Jews from all corners of the globe, in urgent physical danger as well as those seeking spiritual sustenance, would follow in their footsteps to this same tiny sliver of soil, known throughout history as the Holy Land— only now they would come not to die but to live, to build and be rebuilt.

ACKNOWLEDGMENTS

Many thanks to the following for their assistance in providing photos:

American Friends of Hebrew University, Amit, American Technion Society, American Red Magen David, Hadassah, Jewish National Fund, Jewish Week, Na'amat USA. The Gustave Dore illustrations are from the 1866 edition of the Holy Bible, published in London and New York by Cassell, Petter and Galpin.

CONTENTS

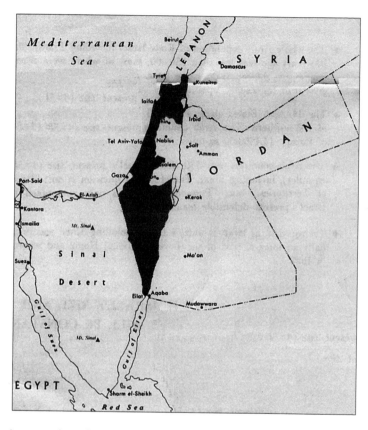

A map of modern Israel. Israel returned the vast Sinai desert to Egypt after the withdrawal following Camp David agreement in 1982. Some 150,000 Jewish settlers live in the West Bank and Gaza Strip.

ISRAEL: THE "HOLY LAND"

Israel has been described as the "Holy Land" for the last two thousand years. Why?

First, for some 3,500 years it has been the homeland of the Jews, promised to them repeatedly by God (in the opening biblical book of Genesis). The civilization that evolved there produced the Jewish religion "Judaism," and this in turn became the mother faith from which two other western religions, Christianity and Islam, sprang. Both faiths are often described as the "daughters" of Judaism.

For Jews who have lived for many generations in the United States, or in any other free country, Israel holds an almost mystical attraction and a very special spiritual bond. This is especially true in the twentieth century which produced, on the one hand, the Holocaust of the Jews in Europe, resulting in the massacre of one-third of the world's Jewish population, and on the other hand, the reborn State of Israel, which has opened its doors to all Jews in urgent need of a safe, secure life.

Consciously or otherwise, Jews remember that the Holocaust murdered six million of their coreligionists, while tiny Israel has welcomed and absorbed more than five million Jews in need and provided a home for an additional one million non-Jews.

Ancient biblical and historic sites, recreated today as modern communities, do not fail to stir the Jews' sense of awe—especially knowing that these ancient towns and cities have lain dormant for nearly two thousand years, following the expulsion of the Jews from their homeland by the Romans.

During the past two millennia of exile, Jews felt a strong sense of kinship with their coreligionists around the globe; at

1

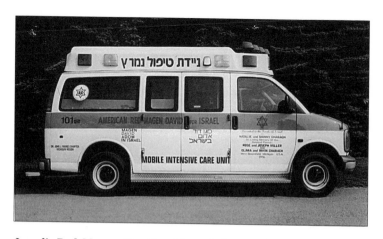

Israel's Red Magen David, with ambulances dotting the country, now features a mobile intensive cardiac care unit.

the same time, they prayed and hoped for the restoration of their homeland, Israel, and even continued to mark its agricultural seasons throughout their long period of exile. Until the Zionist movement was launched towards the end of the 1890s, however, very minuscule numbers of Jews actually believed that Israel would once again become the Jewish homeland.

Today, demographers predict that Israel, in about three or four more decades, will be home to more than two-thirds of the world's Jewish population.

For Christians, Israel is the Holy Land, too, for it is where Jesus was born and raised. Nazareth, Bethlehem (located in the Palestinian area), Galilee, Jerusalem—these are all holy places for Christians.

For Moslems, Israel's capital of Jerusalem is the site where, according to Islamic tradition, Mohammed left the earth and ascended to his heavenly abode astride a white horse.

Jerusalem, both the ancient Old City and the much larger new areas, has a very special quality to which virtually all residents and visitors respond. There is in Jerusalem, and in many other parts of the country, a spiritual ambiance that seeps into people's consciousness, no matter what religion they follow, or even if they are non-believers.

HERZL'S VISION OF THE FUTURE

Theodor Herzl, the founder of the Zionist movement at the beginning of the twentieth century, described his vision of a future Jewish state in these words:

> I believe that a wondrous breed of Jews will spring up from the earth. The Jews who will it shall achieve their own state. We shall live at last as free men and women on our own soil, and in our own homes die peacefully. The world will be liberated by our freedom, enriched by our wealth, magnified by our greatness. Whatever we attempt there for our own benefit will redound mightily and beneficially to the good of all mankind.

For centuries many have described their links to this small land. In the early 1800s, one of the most beloved Hassidic rabbis, Nachman of Bratslav, said: "No matter where I go, it is always to Jerusalem." And many centuries ago, as the tractates of the Talmud were being assembled, Rabbi Zera wrote: "The air of the Land of Israel makes one wise."

On May 14, 1948, the people of Israel declared their independence. Numbering less than 650,000 Jews, they proclaimed: "The Land of Israel was the birthplace of the Jewish people. Here their spiritual, religious and national identity was formed. Here they achieved independence and created a culture of national and universal significance. . . . Impelled by this historic association, Jews strove throughout the centuries to go back to the land of their fathers and regain their statehood."

The Jewish population of Israel has grown in the past half-century to more than five million; the non-Jewish population stands today at about one million. To ensure its security, Israel fought wars in 1948 when invaded by six Arab armies as well as in 1956, 1967 and 1972.

Today Israel is regarded as the strongest power in the Middle East, and the most advanced in science, technology, medicine and education.

FOUR MILLENNIA OF HISTORY

Most historians agree that the Land of Israel was first settled by Abraham, the father of the Jewish people. Often described as the first Jew, Abraham lived with his son Isaac and the third of the patriarchs, Jacob, around 2000 B.C.E. Of course this time frame includes also the four matriarchs—Sarah, Rebecca, Leah and Rachel. The latter two were Jacob's wives; polygamy among Jews was permitted in those days.

Some three hundred to five hundred years later the Israelites, under the leadership of Jacob, proceeded to Egypt because of the famine in Israel. They remained there some four hundred years, first as free men and later as slaves. Around the year 1250,

Moses led the Israelite slaves out of Egypt and back to the Land of Israel, to become free people once again. This exodus is celebrated and recalled today at the Passover holiday.

Under the leadership of Joshua, Moses' right-hand assistant and eventual successor, the former slaves conquered the area known as Canaan, and divided it among the twelve tribes of Israel. After an era of rule by judges, the people copied their neighbors and clamored for a king. About the year 1006 Saul was anointed the first king of Israel. He ruled for some twenty-five years, followed by David, usually acknowledged as Israel's greatest king, who sat on the throne for about forty years. Under David, the hilltop city of Jerusalem became Israel's capital.

Solomon, "the wise king," succeeded David and built the first Holy Temple in Jerusalem. Shortly after Solomon's death, the kingdom split into two—Israel, in the north, comprised ten tribes, while Judea in the south consisted of two (Judah and Benjamin). Some two hundred years later Israel was conquered by Assyria, whose king Sargon II deported all of the inhabitants. These scattered inhabitants are the Ten Lost Tribes often mentioned in historical accounts.

Around 600, the inhabitants of Judah and Benjamin were conquered by the Babylonians, and gradually the captives were exiled to Babylon (now Iraq). In the year 586, on the ninth day of the month of *Av*, (which corresponds to July or August), the Temple was destroyed. Jews still mark this date as a day of fasting and mourning.

King Cyrus of Persia, some seventy years later, defeated the Babylonians and allowed the Jewish captives to return home. Soon after the captives returned to Jerusalem, construction work of the second Holy Temple began. Around 518, the second Temple was completed; it stood as the principal center of worship for the Jews of Israel until the year 70 C.E., when the Romans conquered the country and destroyed the second Temple. The date of the Temple's destruction fell on the ninth of *Av*, just like the first Temple.

The Jews fought the conquering Romans, but were defeated. The punishment for their revolt was exile, which lasted approximately two thousand years until Israel was reestablished in 1948.

In 638 C.E., the Arabs conquered Jerusalem; in 1078, the Turks defeated the Arabs and seized control of the country; in 1096, the First Crusade came and fought the Turks. Tiny pockets of Jewish settlers remained in Israel throughout the centuries, but essentially the entire country slipped into an era of inertia.

The country now called Palestine was ruled by the Turks until 1917 when, during World War I, the British seized the country with the help of a small nucleus of Jews who had settled there following pogroms in Russia. (In the first World War, Turkey sided with Germany and fought against the Allies.) Following the war, the League of Nations assigned Palestine to Britain to be administered as a Mandate.

In 1922 the British cut off some three-quarters of the original territory of Palestine and announced it would become the new Arab state of Transjordan (later changed to Jordan).

Thus, as of 1922 Palestine consisted of the area between the Jordan River and the Mediterranean; in 1917 Britain (later supported by the United States) had issued the Balfour Declaration, pledging a national home in Palestine for the Jewish people. Jews throughout the world saw the Balfour pledge as the beginning of a Jewish return to the ancient homeland.

The wisdom of King Solomon has been passed down through the ages. The dispute between two women who claimed to be the true mother of a baby, and how the king resolved the dispute was captured on canvas by the artist, Dore.

In the 1920s, Jews began to settle in Palestine in sizable numbers. Although few Jews at the time had extensive agricultural or industrial experience, they quickly learned to become efficient farmers, concentrating on citrus crops and a wide variety of other agricultural products. The national council, *Va'ad Leumi*, was formed by the various groups of settlers. Although they had many disagreements, one thing they agreed upon was that they were looking to the future. All of their efforts in reviving the land, in setting up embryonic industrial and commercial enterprises, in organizing collectives (*kibbutzim*), towns and villages, and in developing a school system and health clinics—everything was geared toward the eventual establishment of an infrastructure that would form the foundation of an independent, democratic Jewish state.

An overwhelming percentage of Jewish settlers in the 1920s were Ashkenazic immigrants fleeing the turbulence that prevailed in Russia following the Bolshevik revolution. In addition, the settlers also comprised Jews from Poland, Rumania and Czechoslovakia, many of them motivated by Zionist idealism and others by concern about the growing right-wing fascist organizations. There were also idealistic Zionists who came from the United States and England, including Golda Meir, a future prime minister, who had been raised in Milwaukee.

Other notables who settled in Palestine in this period were the world-famous theologian, Martin Buber, the Nobel Laureate in Literature, Shmuel Agnon, and the lauded Hebrew poet of the twentieth century, Chaim N. Bialik.

By 1933, when Hitler came to power in Germany, the Jewish population of Palestine numbered more than a quarter-million. A city, built on the sand dunes adjacent to ancient, biblical Jaffa, had risen and now seemed to grow almost daily.

Today this city, Tel Aviv, with its suburban towns, is the major modern metropolis in Israel.

The catastrophic events of Nazism in Germany between 1933 and 1939, when Germany launched World War II with its attack on Poland, also brought massive numbers of Jewish immigrants in its wake. First they came from Germany, then from Austria and then—as the dark clouds over Europe became more ominous—from Czechoslovakia, Poland, Rumania and other countries.

Visitors to Israel often enjoy planting tree saplings in the soil.

IMMIGRANTS NOW PROFESSIONALS

Immigrants, especially those from Germany, differed from the Russian and Polish newcomers of earlier years. Those who came in the 1930s were, to a far greater extent, physicians, lawyers, engineers, bankers, and academics who brought their expertise to the still-tiny Jewish community. In the previous decade a university had opened in Jerusalem (the Hebrew University), while in Haifa in the north a modern engineering college had opened (the Technion), and in Tel Aviv a full symphony orchestra had been launched. The refugees fleeing Hitlerism in the 1930s soon found themselves very much needed and appreciated, as they contributed their particular skills to the nascent country and its incipient institutions.

During World War II, immigration to Palestine declined precipitously. The agricultural and industrial products turned out by the Jewish community were of enormous help to the British forces headquartered in nearby Egypt.

Thousands of Palestinian Jews volunteered to fight in the British forces against the Germans, despite the fact that Britain, the mandatory power over Palestine, had sharply curtailed Jewish immigration to the country, a policy outlined in a new White Paper. Most analysts believe that this step was taken in order to keep the Arab countries—with their vast supplies of urgently-needed oil—neutral in the conflict between the Axis and Allied powers.

The Jews who joined the British armed forces did so, remembering the words of David Ben Gurion: "We must assist the British in the war as if there were no White Paper, and we must resist the White Paper as if there were no war."

The Jewish National Fund helped to build reservoirs throughout Israel; it also planted millions of trees during the last eighty years.

A typical classroom at the Hebrew University in Jerusalem.

Many of Israel's military heroes received their early experience on the battlefield while fighting alongside the Allies. The charismatic Moshe Dayan lost his eye while on a secret mission to help the war effort.

The three years between the spring of 1945 and the spring of 1948 were undoubtedly among the most crucial in recent Jewish history. After the Germans surrendered, the world realized, likely for the first time, the extent of the Jewish people's losses—not in war, but as the result of a deliberate government policy of extermination. The numbers were staggering: six million Jews, including one and a half-million children, had been massacred simply because they were Jews.

The remaining twelve million Jews in the world were stunned as they tried to absorb what had happened. Decent people of all faiths were also shocked and unable to grasp the enormity of the crime.

Needless to say, a mood of mourning and depression enveloped the Jewish community. People asked, aloud and silently, *Why? How could this have happened?* Most Jews believed that the world had turned its back on them, ignoring the plight of European Jewry. Some Jews even turned their back on God, spurning all religious and theological explanations for the Holocaust.

The Jews in Palestine had developed over the years into a hard, pragmatic society. They sent emissaries to the United States and to other free countries, delivering a message to fellow Jews: "Mourning and wailing will not help. Whether or not various countries could have prevented the catastrophe is no longer important. We don't want it to happen again. We wish to establish a Jewish homeland, once again, in Palestine which will forever be a refuge for Jews in peril. And we ask you to help."

The Palestinian Jews' message hit home. Depression and grieving gave way to a new era. American and other Jews, and eventually some non-Jews, began to say: "What can we do to help? We will help!"

CLOUDS OF WAR APPEAR

In the postwar era, the old-new state in the making had already experienced sporadic, often violent Arab attacks on the Jewish population. The Jewish leadership looked ahead and realized that some Arab leaders had supported Hitler's forces in the war. The proclamation of a Jewish state would be followed by an all-out assault on the young country—even though the Jews pledged that their future state would offer all citizens equality and liberty.

In the crucial three years following World War II, the Zionist leaders dispatched young Palestinian Jews virtually to every corner of the world with but one mission: "We need arms to defeat the Arab attack that will come as soon as we announce our Jewish state."

The United States, England, France and other western countries had embargoed all arms shipments to the Middle East, fearing another war so soon after the defeat of the Nazis and Japanese. But with the memory of the Holocaust fresh in the minds of most Jews, an unprecedented effort was nevertheless launched to obtain arms.

Secretly, millions of dollars were assembled and made available to companies with innocuous-sounding names, their sole purpose to purchase war surplus supplies and ship them,

Hebrew University students work with computers. The university opened in 1924; the guest speaker at the dedication ceremonies was Albert Einstein.

Aerial view of Hebrew University, located on Mt. Scopus. Arid Judean desert can be seen in the background.

somehow, to the Jews in Palestine. Thousands of Jews in all parts of the United States were involved in this effort, and their secret undertaking remained hidden until many years after Israel was established, and its security guaranteed.

War surplus planes were purchased in the western regions of America, dismantled, and put on secretly-acquired cargo vessels flying false foreign flags. Manned largely by volunteer crews consisting of both Jews and non-Jews, these vessels miraculously succeeded in evading British warships patrolling the Palestinian coast.

One Palestinian Jew, who had a background in engineering, was sent to New York to determine how to build a factory that would be able to turn out small arms ammunition. He was dedicated, hard-working, and had a limited degree of know-how. However, he did not know a word of English. He rented a small room in the old Commodore Hotel, a few blocks from the New York Public Library, on Fifth Avenue.

He soon met a young American Jewish engineer; the only language the two had in common was Yiddish. The Palestinian persuaded the young American to meet him daily at the library, where they spent long hours poring over technical magazines specializing in arms and munitions. One magazine page, or even a photo on a page, would be painstakingly hand-copied by the American.

This went on for days and weeks and months; finally the Palestinian felt he had gathered enough technical data. He thanked his young accomplice, and clutching a bag full of notebooks filled with schematics, photos, graphs (much of it now converted to Hebrew) the Palestinian returned home. Understandably, Israelis are tight-lipped about such information, but it is generally known that a secret ammunition factory was set up and began work—all of it based on the technical data garnered at the library.

ISRAEL'S FIRST THIRTY MONTHS

It was on the afternoon of Friday, May 14, 1948, when members of the National Council gathered in Tel Aviv and listened with tears in their eyes as David Ben Gurion read aloud from Israel's Declaration of Independence, pledging liberty and equality to all citizens and residents, and proclaiming that Israel once again—on its ancestral soil—would be a homeland for the Jewish people. Everyone in the room and the thousands of Jews cheering the streets outside knew that this was a crucial moment and a milestone in the Jewish people's long history.

Six months earlier, at the United Nations headquarters in Lake Success, New York, the General Assembly had voted, by a narrow margin, to divide Palestine into separate Jewish and Arab states. The Jews had accepted the U.N. decision but the Arabs had not, vowing an all-out war.

As the Jews began to absorb the reality of their new status, and to accustom themselves to now being citizens of Israel, the first rumblings of Arab attacks on the new country began. Britain, the Mandatory Power, had pulled out of the country just hours earlier. Israel's military leaders knew how sparse the country's defenses were.

Virtually every able-bodied man, and large numbers of women, were recruited in the fledgling army. Not only were there not enough uniforms, but even guns—any kind of weapon—were at a premium.

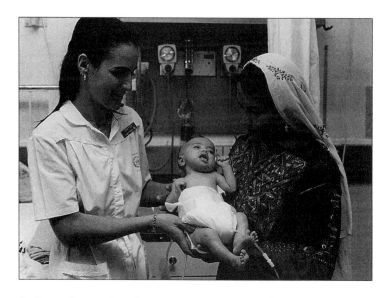

In Jerusalem, a Jewish nurse assists a new Bedouin mother.

Today, agriculture in Israel is among the most advanced in the world; often it is aided by computers. In this 1920s photo, early Jewish pioneers sow the soil in primitive style—by hand.

David Ben Gurion, generally called the "architect of Israel," was the first prime minister, guiding the country through its difficult early years.

Within hours of Israel's proclamation of independence, the United States announced its formal recognition of the new state. President Truman swept away the objections of his own State Department, and wished the country every success. Within hours, too, immigrants began to pour into Israel, arriving at the bustling port of Haifa, then the only major site of embarkation in the country. Many immigrants had been interned on the island of Cyprus for months, because they had tried to break the British embargo on Jewish immigration to Palestine. The overwhelming majority of these arrivals were survivors of the Holocaust.

As soon as they arrived, the younger and stronger men were drafted into the Israeli army, which was still being formed from the pre-state Haganah underground defense force. Although the new recruits hardly knew any Hebrew, and few of them had any weapons, they all felt that, against overwhelming odds, this tiny country was their last chance of ever having a normal, free life. Whatever this un-uniformed, weapons-shy, ragtag army lacked, they more than made up for in courage, enthusiasm and devotion.

During the next few months, Israel fought against six Arab countries, all of whom were equipped with modern arms and trained by experienced officers. When the ceasefires gave way to a permanent armistice under the watchful eye of the United Nations, the stream of immigrants now became a flood. In addition to Holocaust survivors, large numbers of Jews were compelled to flee from their homes in Arab countries.

Generally this tidal wave of immigration was composed of poor Jews who had eked out a minimal livelihood as farmers, craftsmen and shopkeepers. The Israelis' dramatic success in defeating the combined Arab assaults had produced reactions of fury and frustration in many Arab countries. Mobs, often encouraged by government officials, attacked and threatened their Jewish populations, notwithstanding the fact that Jews had been living in those countries peacefully for many centuries. After the defeat of their armies by the Israelis, the Jews in the Arab world were now often described as spies and traitors.

From the North African countries most of the Jewish newcomers to Israel reached Israel by sea, usually with nothing more than the clothes on their backs. From more distant Yemen and Iraq they came by air, on planes that bore the identity of fictitious companies, often flown by non-Jewish crews.

During the three years between May 1948 and approximately May 1951, the Jewish population of Israel exploded from 650,000 to about one and a half million. By and large the new arrivals were either survivors of the European Holocaust who wanted to get far away from the blood-soaked lands where their families had been brutally massacred, or they were poor Jews from Moslem countries fleeing for their lives.

All of the newcomers knew that life in Israel was not going to be easy, but they were determined to build new lives for themselves, and especially for their children. Jewish communities in every part of the free world, notably in the United States, launched massive campaigns in the late 1940s and 1950s until the end of the century to help Israel through this period.

At first, as the immigrants arrived, the only housing available to them were tin huts, tents and wooden shacks. A single faucet, hooked up to the area water system, served hundreds of newcomers. Food was in short supply and rationing was instituted. Nobody went hungry, but they had to live on imported frozen fish from Scandinavia for over a year, and be content with an egg or two a week.

By the hundreds of thousands, Jewish immigrants poured into Israel in the early 1950s. They were survivors of the Holocaust, and Jews from Moslem countries. For a few difficult years the only housing available were tents, shown here.

Life in the temporary tent cities in the early 1950s was difficult. Shown is the Tiberias ma'abara, *a transit camp.*

Jewish immigrants from Morocco streamed into Israel in the early 1950s, despite reports of inadequate housing, jobs and foodstuffs.

Permanent housing had to be created, jobs had to be made available to unskilled workers, schools had to be built, and hospitals had to be set up. The newcomers had to learn Hebrew, and to feel themselves part and parcel of a free, new country. And, of course, Israel had to maintain maximum alertness in maintaining its defenses.

The temporary homes, which were too cold in winter and too hot in summer, gradually gave way to modern, permanent apartments. Some newcomers opted to settle on new farming settlements in remote parts of the country, while others chose to learn factory skills and live in the large urban centers. The early years of Israel's history were very difficult; mistakes in planning were made, and were later rectified.

Certain European newcomers were able to adapt themselves to areas inhabited primarily by Jews from the Arab world; but, in some cases, there were clashes—cultural, social clashes. Slowly and steadily, life in Israel improved in terms of housing, health facilities, food, jobs, and opportunities for higher education.

Today, at the beginning of the twenty-first century, Israel is no longer a Third World country. Per capita income in the country is on a par with that of England. There is compulsory education for every youngster, free of charge. Because of Israel's diverse population, there are four types of schools: non-religious, religious, yeshivas, and Arab. In addition to the traditional curriculum found in schools all over the free world, the schools in Israel, both religious and non-religious, teach Bible on a regular basis.

An aerial view of the vast Ein Karem Medical Center in Jerusalem, open to all and supported by Hadassah.

Rina Mor, shown here in her army uniform, won the Miss Universe title in 1976.

HIGHER EDUCATION EXPANDS

Israel also takes pride in its institutions of higher learning. The Hebrew University in Jerusalem, the oldest in the country with a medical school, is often described as the finest in the Middle East; Ben Gurion University in Beersheba emphasizes conservation and desert fructification; Tel Aviv University is a general institution with the largest student body in the country; Bar-Ilan University, located in Ramat Gan, a Tel Aviv suburb, combines Judaic studies with general material; Haifa University is a general institution in the north with a large number of Arab students; Technion, also in Haifa, is usually described as the "M.I.T. of Israel," as it specializes in engineering and technology; Weizmann Institute in Rehovot, between Jerusalem and Tel Aviv, does not have a large student body—but it is now regarded as one of the world's leading research centers. In all, more than 60,000 students are enrolled in Israel's universities.

One thing quickly becomes apparent when you visit an Israeli university: the students all seem older than other countries' university students. Generally speaking they are, since the vast majority begin their university studies after they have first completed military service. Thus, a freshman is often twenty-one years old; quite a few students attend classes in military uniform, since they may be studying specific subjects as part of their service.

In addition to university students, there are tens of thousands of young Orthodox Jews who continue their yeshiva studies well into their twenties. Some ten thousand American students, mostly but not all Jewish, are enrolled in Israeli universities and yeshivas in any given year. For this reason, some courses are taught in English.

Technion-Israel Institute of Technology in Haifa is often called the "M.I.T. of Israel." Most of Israel's engineers, technologists, architects and scientists are Technion alumni. Pictured, a lecture hall.

Three Technion students try to solve a problem together.

There exists in Israel a very special and unique reverence for the Bible. Most Jews, through the centuries, have considered it their greatest contribution to humanity. And David Ben Gurion who studied Bible regularly with some of Israel's greatest scholars, commented: "We have preserved the Book, and the Book has preserved us."

GEOGRAPHY/ ENVIRONMENT/ REGIONS

Even a cursory glance at the map of Israel indicates its unique geographical location. Situated at the eastern end of the Mediterranean, technically in the continent of Asia, Israel is usually considered part of the Middle East. It is also at the junction of three vast continents: Asia, Africa and Europe.

Because of Israel's strategic position, it has been the site of fierce, bloody battles between various bellicose countries throughout the centuries. Today, Israel is surrounded by five Moslem nations: Lebanon, in the north; Syria, in the northeast; Jordan, in the east; Egypt, in the southwest; and Saudi Arabia in the southeast, which lies along the Gulf of Eilat, as do Israel, Jordan and Egypt.

From the northernmost point to its southernmost point in Eilat, the whole country is 280 miles long, and thus can be traversed by a steady drive in less than a day. The widest area in Israel stretches some 85 miles, while the narrowest area, between the sea and the tentative border of the West Bank Arab region, is a mere 14 miles. The distance between its two principal cities, Jerusalem, the capital, and Tel Aviv, is only an hour's drive.

As small as Israel is, it nevertheless has an amazingly wide variety of climates. In the extreme north, along strategic Mount Hermon, you can go skiing. If so inclined, you can proceed to Lake Kinneret next, also called the Sea of Galilee, for some swimming, boating or fishing. Conceivably you could then proceed a little more southward and go kayaking on the Jordan River. And then, if you are really ambitious, you could drive south to the Dead Sea, for a chance to float in this remarkable body of water—the lowest spot on earth, estimated at 1,300 feet below sea level.

Israel's variegated weather is the result of vastly different land regions: in the southern Negev desert, the sands may be burning, while the mountain tops in the northern Galilee region are covered with snow. Along the long coast of Israel, the winters are relatively mild and the summers enjoy cooling breezes. Some forty miles inland is the Jordan Valley, a humid, hot area where temperatures of 110 degrees are not uncommon.

Israel is usually described as having only two seasons, because the summers tend to be hot and the winters rainy and cold, especially in the higher elevations. The summers in Israel are so devoid of rain that car owners remove their windshield wipers for months at a time. There is one weather phenomenon in Israel that usually occurs in late spring or early summer: a hot, dusty wind that engulfs everyone and everything for a day or two, enervating most before blowing away. It is usually called by its Arabic name, *chamsin*.

At the peak of the summer months, people tend to go to work early, when the air is relatively cool; they then take a break between noon and three o'clock in the afternoon, returning to work for a few hours later. However, this system, which also extends to banks, government offices and large retail shops, is gradually disappearing as modern air conditioning is being introduced to more establishments.

Theodor Herzl, often called "King of the Jews," founded the modern Zionist movement at the end of the nineteenth century.

Students in the Amit school, a modern religious institution, shown lining up for their trip home by bus.

Young Amit school students learn to master the computer.

The regions of Israel are usually divided into six areas: the Negev desert which occupies sixty percent of Israel's territory, in the south; the coastal plain along the Mediterranean, with Lebanon in the extreme north and Egypt at its southern tip; the fertile Jezreel Valley, just south of the verdant Galilee; the Central Mountains, in Israel's center and including the Galilee; the Jordan Rift, from the northern border to Eilat, adjoining the Jordan River (which actually continues on to Africa); and the Four Seas of Israel—the Mediterranean in the west, the Jordan River emptying into the fabled Dead Sea, Lake Kinneret in the north which doubles as Israel's vital source of potable water, and the Gulf of Eilat in the south which leads to the Indian Ocean.

The Bible asserts that ancient Israel was a country rich in a wide variety of flora and fauna. The hills were lush with forests, and the valleys full with blooming flowers. During the Jewish people's two millennia of exile, the land was virtually abandoned, and embattled armies used the country to stage their wars. Thus, when Jews began their return to Israel a little over a century ago, they found to their dismay that the natural environment was in shambles.

Today there is in Israel a strong, organized movement to transform the country once again into a "land flowing with milk and honey." Green, well-tended parks of all shapes and sizes abound throughout the country. On Friday afternoon, as families prepare for the traditional Sabbath eve dinner generally attended by all family members, flowers dominate the pre-dinner shopping. Since their return to Israel, the Jews there have developed a passion for the beauty and naturalness of multi-colored flowers.

Throughout the country there are some three hundred nature preserves designed to protect the landscape, conserve the quality of air and water, and guard the animals, plants and birds that are native to the region. The Jewish National Fund, now approaching its second century of work, has devoted itself to draining swampy land in Israel, planting trees in every corner of the country, building reservoirs, and initiating other related programs. The first collectives (*kibbutzim*) and early industrial sites were erected on land purchased and reclaimed by this group. To date the J.N.F. has planted more than 200 million trees, and made available hundreds of parks and picnic sites in Israel for people to enjoy.

Some of the nature preserves have brought, from various parts of the world, rare species of animals mentioned in the Bible. One such creature is the ibex, now beginning to populate in Israel. This mountain-climbing member of the goat family has unusually long horns.

A recently revived ancient Israeli custom involves newborns. Whenever possible, a cypress tree is planted when a girl is born and a cedar tree for a boy. When these children marry their spouses, branches are cut from the grown trees and are used for the traditional wedding canopy (the *huppah*).

One unusual holiday that characterizes Jews' admiration for trees is known as Tu B'Shvat, occurring on the fifteenth day of the month *Shvat* (usually in March). This date, cited in the Talmud, is also known as New Year's Day for Trees. In Israel, school children, adults and visitors disperse to specific areas in the countryside and plant tree saplings provided by the J.N.F. Outside of Israel, children are encouraged to provide funds for tree planting. It is also customary, in Israel and overseas, to celebrate this unique festival by eating fruit indigenous to Israel, for example figs and dates.

The Bible cautioned against destroying fruit trees. In times of war, the ancient Israelites were told, "You may eat of them, but you may not cut them down."

JERUSALEM: THE ANCIENT CAPITAL

Three thousand years ago, when the charismatic King David ruled, he made Jerusalem the capital of the Jewish homeland. During those three millennia, Jerusalem has never ceased being the focus of the Jewish people, who remained in exile for two-thirds of that long stretch of time.

Today, for Jews, Christians, Moslems, as well as for followers of other faiths, Jerusalem is still a holy city—modern yet ancient, entirely spiritual yet pragmatic and down to earth. In ancient Israel, especially when the Holy Temple was the focus of nationwide worship, prophets and kings preached and ruled. A resident or visitor today soon grows accustomed to the daily scene: rabbis, priests, nuns, scholars, students, Jewish and Arab families, and Christian tourists from every corner of the world. They come to worship, to study, to visit the Holy Sites, and to absorb the city's unique spiritual atmosphere. Fridays, Saturdays and Sundays are especially busy since these are the Sabbath days of Moslems, Jews and Christians respectively. Stand near the plaza facing the Western Wall where the Holy Temple once stood and you will see large numbers of Jews praying at the sacred site, many of them stuffing little pieces of paper into the wall's cracks and asking for the recovery of an ill loved one. Close by is the gold-topped Mosque of Omar where Moslems assemble to pray. Not far away, both in the Old City which is an ancient enclave within the new Jerusalem and in the city proper, many hundreds of synagogues, churches and mosques attract thousands of worshipers.

In 1948, when Israel proclaimed its independence and withstood the attacks of six Arab nations, Jordan took the Old City. It was held until 1967 when, during the course of the lightning Six Day War, the Israelis captured it.

In ancient days, a priest would stand on a roof and blow hard on a *shofar*, a ram's horn, to announce the arrival of the Sabbath. Nowadays in some of the more Orthodox areas of Jerusalem, the approaching Sabbath is announced on a modern siren. Church bells are heard almost constantly, as well as the call to prayer to Moslems that the *muezzin* issues, now usually amplified by an audio tape player.

Israel's parliament, the Knesset, is housed in Jerusalem, as are the official residences of its president and prime minister. The Supreme Court is headquartered here, and the Hebrew University and Hadassah Hospital are also located in Jerusalem. There are industrial parks both within and outside of the city where small and medium-size companies produce their varied products, often in the field of technology.

There are, of course, tens of thousands of yeshiva students, both young and old, pursuing their religious and secular studies. During the past three decades, the City has become the world's leading center for Jewish scholarly books and periodicals.

Despite its small size, Israel usually occupies a disproportionately large amount of space in the daily newspaper. There are formal peace pacts between Israel and Egypt and Jordan; nevertheless there are occasional acts of terrorism carried out by extremist Arab groups. Despite this, visitors and residents alike insist that walking through the streets of Jerusalem, Tel Aviv or any urban area, day or night, holds no fear for them.

41

Modern Tel Aviv, with marina, breakwater and boardwalk, also features shorefront luxury hotels.

Before trees can be planted, the saplings must be grown and nurtured.

There is a sense of safety and security that is often absent in other metropolitan communities.

As always, Israel continues to remain a land of sharp contrasts and remarkable paradoxes. Arab patients come to Israel's ultra-modern hospitals, sometimes in great secrecy, to regain their health. And yet at the same time members of those same families may commit violent political acts against Jews. The biblical prophecy that "in blood and fire Judea fell and in blood and fire Judea will arise" certainly seems borne out.

One of the world's newest countries, Israel is also one of the world's oldest. Small in size and with less people than the populations of many major cities, Israel is already a world leader in the field of technology. A portion of its ultra-Orthodox citizens insist on dressing as though they still lived in eighteenth-century Poland. They can be seen wearing long sidelocks, as well as fur trimmed hats.

There are sharp differences of interpretation within the Jewish community as to what constitutes religious observance. Israel, by virtue of the fact that more than eighty percent of its population is Jewish, observes Saturday as its Sabbath day of rest. The large hotels, the Israel defense forces, government offices, and the national airline, El Al, all observe the kosher dietary laws.

Native-born Israelis are called *sabras*, meaning a prickly pear that is tough and thorny on the outside, but once opened its insides are sweet. The Israelis assert that they are like the *sabra* because of the tensions with which they live. They also note that Arab antagonism has had positive results for them: the decades-long Arab boycott has forced Israel to create products which, with positive effects, have helped to make the country economically self-sufficient.

Technical high schools, sponsored by Na'amat, provide students with unique educational opportunities.

Ethiopian, Russian and Israeli youngsters study scientific farming at the Kanot Agricultural High School.

Hebrew University students receive their grades.

The chief aspect of Israel that makes it unique is its people. Not only is Israel the only Jewish country in the world where Judaism is the majority religion, but it is also the country with the largest number of Holocaust survivors and their offspring. Jews from the Arab world who found refuge there a half-century ago have now been joined by a large number of Jews from the former Soviet Union who have also fled anti-Semitism to build new lives in Israel. Tens of thousands of Jews from Ethiopia as well as an even larger number of Jews from Latin America have opted to start their lives anew in Israel.

Nevertheless, more than sixty percent of the Israeli population is native-born. Most of the immigrants who settled in Israel knew a Jewish language usually spoken by their own community: Yiddish was widespread in eastern Europe, Ladino was the language of the Sephardic Jews, Judeo-Arabic was brought by newcomers from the Arab countries, and Amharic was spoken by the Ethiopians. Miraculously, the ancient Hebrew language, the language of the Bible, which had been used for some two millennia for prayer and study, was revived and modernized—thanks primarily to the stubborn efforts of one man, Eliezer Ben Yehuda, beginning over a century ago.

Ben Yehuda's vision was that Hebrew would unify the people and the country, and this vision has since been realized. There is a National Language Council that meets in Jerusalem to coin new words, often based on ancient biblical of talmudic terms, to meet the needs of a modern society.

Once a visitor becomes accustomed to Israel's unique way of life, he or she soon begins to recognize two characteristics of Judaism that have become part and parcel of Israeli life: the supreme emphasis on the value of each and every person, and the love that is shown for learning and knowledge. Israelis seem to be harking back to prophetic days when they openly complain and criticize government actions. This calls to mind the ancient prophets who did not hesitate to speak to kings and priests sharply when they thought that a reprimand was called for.

To demonstrate how rapidly the day-to-day situation in Israel changes, some twenty-five years ago, most Jews in the world believed that the Jews in the Soviet Union were "lost." They had been deprived of Jewish religious and cultural life under the Soviets for so long that in another generation or two, it was thought that most of them would disappear into the far greater Russian society. Now, however, these Russian Jews make up a full twenty percent of Israel's Jewish population.

S.Y. Agnon, Israel's Nobel Laureate in Literature.

The nineteenth-century French artist, Gustave Dore, depicted hundreds of biblical stories, including those recounting the very early years of the Israelites. Shown here is the universally-known story of David and Goliath.

TWO MILLENNIA OF HISTORY

To fully understand the historical background of Israel, one must have a grasp of two essentials: first, what happened in the Land of Israel proper after the Romans forcibly expelled the Jews; and second, what happened to the Jews during their long exile virtually extending to every corner of the world.

Incensed that the Jews in the Land of Israel would dare rebel against the mighty Roman empire, the Romans, in the year 70 C.E. destroyed the Holy Temple in Jerusalem and exiled an overwhelming majority of the Jews. Today, some Jewish communities in remote parts of Asia and Europe claim that they have lived in these areas ever since their ancestors were first resettled there by the Romans.

The Romans changed the name of the country from its traditional designation as the Land of Israel, or *Eretz Israel* in Hebrew, to Palestine in honor of the Philistines who occupied a narrow stretch of coastal territory around what is today the modern Israeli city of Ashkelon. The name Palestine remained for the last two millennia, even among Jewish communities. Indeed, in the first half of the twentieth century, the early Jewish settlers referred to themselves as Palestinian Jews. The terms Israel and Israelis were revived when the State of Israel was founded in May 1948.

In his classic history of the Jews and their war against the Romans, Josephus wrote that in destroying Jerusalem the Romans killed one million Jews. Tens of thousands of Jews were captured and sold into slavery. Every town and village in Israel was subjected to the Romans' brutal attacks. The loss of one million Jews during the Romans' wars against the Jews in their

51

homeland brings to mind an observation by the noted Jewish historian, Cecil Roth: "The Jewish people, a very ancient people," he wrote, "would number today at least 100 million had it not been for two millennia of pogroms, massacres, attacks, expulsions and forced conversions."

The Romans believed in a scorched earth policy. Fruit trees were cut down, farming areas were uprooted, and cities and villages were devastated—each a form of intimidation and vengeance. On the other hand, Pliny wrote that the Jewish soldiers, not wishing the Roman troops to benefit from the country's crops, destroyed many of the trees themselves. The Romans, in fits of rage, forbade the Jews from practicing their religious observances, resulting in a state of demoralization for the Jews—a situation similar to that of the Jews in the Soviet Union who were prohibited from all Jewish religious observances.

Descendants of King David were searched out and killed; this was to eliminate the Jewish tradition that the Davidic kingdom would continue and the Jewish dynasty would come to an end. A harsh tax was imposed on all Jews—men, women and children—to be used for the Roman god, Jupiter. The Jews interpreted this as a form of coercive idolatry.

During the first three centuries, life in Israel under Roman rule continued with enormous hardships for the Jews. Sporadic rebellious outbreaks by the Jews were followed by even more repressive measures. Whatever religious life existed was conducted secretly and with great fear. This era corresponded to the early years of Christianity, whose new adherents sought to convince the Jews to join the new faith. It was a period of spiritual as well as political turmoil, not only in Israel but throughout the world.

In the seventh century, there was a major change: the expanding Persian empire planned to defeat and replace the Romans throughout the Middle East. In 614 the Persians entered Israel and proceeded to capture city after city, often with the help of Jewish forces. The Jews saw in the Persians' arrival a ray of hope that Roman subjugation would soon come to an end.

In the same year that the Persians seized Jerusalem, they handed the city to the Jews who began to resettle there and remove the Christian churches. The Persian-Jewish accord lasted some three years; in 622 the Byzantines attacked the Persians, forcing them out of Israel. Seven years later, presumably under pressure by the Church, the Byzantines expelled the Jews from Jerusalem. Many Jews were killed, others fled the country.

ARAB CONQUEST BEGINS

Arab tribesmen began their conquest of the Land of Israel and the area of what is today Syria in the middle of the seventh century. They arrived mainly from the northwestern region of modern-day Saudi Arabia. The so-called Arab Period of Israel continued until 1099, and commenced shortly after Mohammed came on the scene, launching his new religious faith, Islam.

In accordance with Islamic teaching and tradition, the Arabs sought to convert the local population to the new faith. Most of the inhabitants during this period were by now Christians, the Jews having been exiled or having left the country. By the ninth century, Arabic influence began to wane, as Turkish princes arrived. They battled the Arabs and then fought amongst themselves.

By the end of the first millennium, incursions into the Jewish homeland had become commonplace. The Ummayads and the Qays dominated for a time controlling specific areas of Israel, the latter group spreading out especially in the Galilee and Golan. Ahmed ibn Tulun, a Turkish prince, established an independent monarchy in Egypt in 868, which was followed by a takeover of ancient Israel and Syria a decade later. The next Islamic group to rule was made up of the Fatimids and the Byzantines, but the latter were driven back to the territory they occupied in Syria.

Between 1024 and 1029, Bedouin tribes succeeded in defeating the Fatimids and taking control of the country. Around this time a Turkish people called the Seljuks began their first forays into the area. They captured Jerusalem and nearly the rest of Israel in the middle of the eleventh century. However, soon after, about a year before the first Crusaders entered the Holy Land, the Fatimids seized the country. Bitter internecine fighting between the main groupings of Islam, the Sunnis and the Shi'ites erupted. There were small groups of Jewish agricultural colonies in the area around Jericho and the city of Eilat. The advent of the Crusades soon put an end to these hold-out Jewish settlements.

THE CRUSADES

In the year 1095 Pope Urban issued an appeal to fellow Christians to come to the rescue of the Holy Land and safeguard it for the world's Christians. His appeal met with an immediate response. Peasants, largely illiterate, were formed into roving bands across Europe—from Germany, Hungary and the Balkans—and their destination was the Holy Land. En route they came across defenseless Jewish villages and communities and destroyed them.

But this mob of peasants never reached their destination. When they finally entered Turkish territory, the Turkish military forces attacked and killed them. Nonetheless, the Pope's appeal was answered a few years later when a new crusade set out, composed this time of organized, military forces, many of them protected by body armor. They sailed to Lebanon, and from there headed south on the coastal road. Fearful of the Crusaders, the residents of Caeserea furnished them with provisions. In Ramleh the inhabitants were even more terrified of what lay in store for them; they fled, abandoning the once-flourishing city.

When the Crusaders reached Jerusalem, their primary goal, they besieged the city; six weeks later, the city surrendered. The invaders killed an estimated 30,000 people, largely Jews. Some Jews were captured and sold as slaves to Italy, while a handful of others managed to escape to Egypt.

After the fall of Jerusalem, most other cities quickly surrendered to the Crusaders. Moslem populations from traditionally Arab communities like Jaffa, Nablus and Jericho fled in all directions. Jaffa became the Crusaders' principal gateway to the Holy Land. Year after year the conquerors continued to consolidate their hold on the Holy Land. It took nearly a century before they also seized control of what is today Jordan.

By 1170 a new historical figure arose: Saladin of Egypt was mobilizing Moslem forces to oust the Crusaders. Fierce battles raged throughout the area—in Gaza, Galilee, Eilat and elsewhere—and by 1291, after two centuries of the Crusaders' hegemony in the Holy Land, their rule came to an end. Under peace treaties between the Moslems and Christians, the latter were allowed to make regular pilgrimages to Jerusalem. while a

Crusader region was permitted to remain between Jaffa northward to Tyre (today a part of Lebanon).

During the next hundred years, the Holy Land was tossed around like a Ping-Pong ball: Frederick, emperor of Germany, proclaimed himself king of Jerusalem, and then returned to Europe. Additional crusades arrived, waged war with various Moslem armies, sometimes built impressive fortresses, and then returned home. A large Turkish army, fleeing from the Mongols in the east, reached Jerusalem, captured the city and fought off attempts by Egypt to annex parts of the Holy Land. Eventually the Mamluks arrived—a strong, militaristic Egyptian class— and ruled the Holy Land after the rout of the Crusaders in 1291. The Mamluks dominated the country until 1516.

During these years small pockets of Jews had remained as residents. At times the minuscule Jewish population had joined forces with the Moslems and the Fatimids against the Crusaders, particularly when reports of wholesale killing of Jews circulated, both in the Holy Land and the Diaspora lands from which the conquerors came. Some Jews believed the bloody battles were a prelude to the Messianic era. In the late nineteenth century, letters were found in a Cairo synagogue dating back from the thirteenth to the fifteenth centuries, describing the efforts of Jews to rescue their coreligionists—some of whom were held for ransom and others in peril of being slaughtered.

Historical records note that four small communities—Tyre and Banias in the north, and Ashkelon and Rafa in the south— took in Jews fleeing from the Crusaders. Handfuls of other Jews managed to reach temporary safety in Egypt. Despite the hardships of the tiny Jewish community, a few of the Crusaders, notably Obadiah who came from Normandy, converted to the Jewish faith. The only city in the country where the Crusaders forbade Jews to take up residence was Jerusalem, which was, of course, their holiest city and the Jewish homeland's religious and political capital.

As the power of the Christian Crusaders began to fade, and the Mamluks began their dominion of the country, lasting to the middle of the sixteenth century, small groups of Jews from various European areas—persecuted by Crusaders and peasants alike—began to trickle back to the Jewish homeland. Mostly they moved to Acre and, for those who could obtain special permission, to Jerusalem. The growing power of Saladin encouraged the oppressed Jews to hope that a better life would await them in the Land of Israel. Indeed, Saladin later issued a call to world Jewry to settle in the Holy City of Jerusalem. According to one document, three hundred rabbis from France and England soon took up residence in Jerusalem, and began teaching and studying there.

However, the good news did not last long. Jerusalem was attacked and destroyed by a Turkish force in 1244; presumably the Jews left in the city met their death at that time. Nevertheless, the great biblical scholar Nahmanides made his way to Jerusalem from his home in France, and in the latter years of the thirteenth century lived in Jerusalem and Acre. During his sojourn in the Holy Land, he completed his classic commentary on the Torah, the first Five Books of the Hebrew Bible. A grandson of Maimonides, David ben Abraham also lived in Acre for many years.

In 1291 Acre was conquered, and its sparse Jewish community was reduced to ashes. The Jews of that time were mostly artisans, concentrating on dyeing and blowing glass. There were also a few wealthy Jews who were ship owners and international traders, but they were few and far between.

THE MAMLUK PERIOD

When relative peace and quiet were restored to the country under the Moslem rule of the Mamluks, there was simultaneously a decline in the Holy Land's role in world affairs. Internecine fighting broke out among the various Arab chieftains in the Holy Land, and this carried over to the Syrian territory. During these battle-scarred years, political changes in the area were introduced which lasted for brief periods, and later were supplanted by new changes. Gaza, for example, was declared independent; Damascus, the capital of Syria, was given control of Galilee cities for a time. Meanwhile, still fearful of renewed Crusader attempts on the Holy Land, the Mamluks destroyed both the major and minor coastal cities of Jaffa, Acre and several others.

According to a number of historical records, the chief products being grown and processed in the country were olive oil and olive oil soap. One account noted that the poorest of the local population were some seventy Jewish families, who had no visible means of support and provisions. Gradually the whole country became a fundamentalist, orthodox Moslem entity. One Christian church, for instance, was subjected to strong criticism for seeking to enlarge its premises. Moslems argued forcibly with the handful of Jews over the latter's legal right to a synagogue.

Plagues, including one biblical-style locust plague, as well as earthquakes struck the country repeatedly in the fifteenth century. Most local residents now hoped that that Turkish Ottoman empire would drive the Mamluks back to Egypt, so that perhaps the Jews' and Moslems' deteriorating economic lot would improve.

Jews in Europe—those exiled descendants of the Jews expelled from their homeland by the Romans—started to trickle back to the Holy Land. They found the return extremely difficult; coastal cities destroyed by the Mamluks to prevent the Crusaders' return were now unavailable to the tiny Jewish community, which generally prospered in an urban setting where they could ply their artisan skills. Groups of Jews spread out as far as modern Jordan, although most gravitated to Jerusalem.

A dispute erupted between the Pope and the Christian enclave in the Holy Land; they opposed the minute Jewish community in Jerusalem. The cause: Who had the rights to King David's (alleged) tomb on Mount Zion in Jerusalem, the Christians or the Jews? At one point in the controversy the Pope decreed that "Christian ships" should not transport Jews to the Holy Land. One historian of the time wrote that in response to the Pope's edict, Jews nevertheless sought to reach the Holy Land overland from Europe, traveling "from Nuremberg to Posen to Lemberg to Akerman [on the shore of the Black Sea] to Samsun, in Turkey, to Tukat, Aleppo, Damascus, to Jerusalem."

In the years prior to the expulsion of the Jews from Spain in 1492—a cataclysmic event since the Spanish Jewish community had been supremely prosperous, secure and advanced—small groups of Jews had made their way to the historic Jewish homeland. Some of these immigrants apparently were *conversos,* Jews of Spain and Portugal who had converted to the Catholic faith so as to avoid persecution by the church but who practiced Judaism secretly. Once they reached the Holy Land, they reverted to their original faith without fear. Some of these newcomers settled in Gaza, and others in Kfar Kana near Nazareth, and still others in Safed.

In Jerusalem the economic situation of the Jews was severe, largely because of crushing taxes. Many Jews, both Sephardic and Ashkenazic, moved to other parts of the country. The few who remained supported themselves as artisans—as strap makers, smiths, weavers and spice traders. One historian of the period, Obadiah of Bertinoro, wrote that relations between ordinary Moslems and Jews were good, but noted that the pursuit of Judaic studies had declined enormously.

Under Suleiman the Magnificent, the Holy Land was redivided, with four major districts; Jerusalem, Gaza, Nablus and Safed. Political and economic conditions improved, and the agricultural yield became greater and more varied, with dates, figs, apples, pears and other fruits and vegetables appearing in the street vendors' stalls. The country's population increased and the still small Jewish community concentrated on cloth-dyeing and wine production. Power for manufacturing purposes came from windmills.

Between 1521 and 1522 there were some three hundred Jewish families in Jerusalem, according to a report of the period by Rabbi Moses Basola. Widows were not included in this census and were exempt from taxation. The small community, Basola reported, was augmented by Spanish Jewish refugees fleeing the Inquisition. Some two hundred impoverished Jews were supported by charity, donated mostly from Jews living abroad.

JEWS NUMBER 5,000 IN THE 16TH CENTURY

In the mid-sixteenth century there were an estimated one thousand Jewish families—approximately five thousand people—living in the Holy Land; some were Ashkenazic, having arrived largely from central Europe, some were Sephardim, refugees from the Inquisition's expulsion, and others were Jews from North

African lands. Still others, although few in number, had descended from families living in remote corners of the country who had never left, despite the Romans' edicts for all Jews to be expelled.

These Jews resided in Nablus (Shechem), Safed, Hebron and in various Galilee villages, including Peki'in whose Jews had never left the village from Roman times. Many of the newcomers settled in Safed which soon became an important commercial and industrial center. Its Jewish population gradually grew to an estimated ten thousand; over time it also became a major religious center. Among the famous rabbis who were ordained in Safed during this period were Joseph Caro who wrote the classic *Shulchan Aruch,* which remains to this day a staple of Jewish scholarship.

Safed also emerged as the Jewish world's center of *Kabbalah* (Jewish mysticism), and today remains a center for mystical studies. Rabbi Isaac Luria, known as the Ari, taught in Safed and made it his base.

During this period especially, Jews yearned strongly for messianic redemption, and beliefs soon developed in the Diaspora and in some of the Holy Land regions that redemption was at hand. Tiberias, located on the shores of Lake Kinneret (Sea of Galilee), had been virtually devastated by earthquakes. In response to growing messianic hopes, one of the great Jewish women of history, Dona Gracia Nasi, who was extraordinarily wealthy, obtained permission from the governing sultan to rebuild the city. Construction began, but after a number of years it was abandoned.

In the final years of the sixteenth century, Jews living in Safed and Galilee towns suffered from an outbreak of banditry carried out by Bedouin and Druze tribes. These tribes sought to take advantage of the presumed wealth of those Jews engaged in commercial and industrial pursuits.

This Jewish family came to Israel from the Soviet Union in 1990. More than one million Russian Jews—twenty percent of the Jewish population—have settled in Israel.

Picnic areas are popular spots in hundreds of parks throughout Israel.

The Safed Jewish community, continually terrorized by acts of banditry, began to dwindle; many Jews moved to the nearby island of Cyprus. Meanwhile, by the end of the seventeenth century, records show that a desolate Tiberias was completely bereft of a single Jewish resident. The Jerusalem Jewish community now began to suffer from the cruel taxes imposed by the tyrannical Bedouin sheikh, Muhammad ibn Faroukh, who ruled the city.

The Jerusalem Jews, in times of great difficulty in the Holy City, often would find temporary respite by moving to Hebron or Gaza until conditions improved. Around 1648-1649, small groups of Jews from Ukraine began to arrive in Jerusalem, seeking refuge from the terrible pogroms that had broken out in their towns and villages under the direction of the notorious Cossack leader, Bogdan Chmelnicki. Although the attacks were ostensibly aimed at ending Polish rule in Ukraine, three hundred Jewish communities were ultimately destroyed and 100,000 Jews were killed by the Cossack bands.

NAPOLEON INVADES THE HOLY LAND

Until Napoleon arrived in the late eighteenth century, the Holy Land's condition fluctuated. Turks and Egyptian Moslems vied for control and the chance to impose taxes; at times they fought each other, and at other times they formed alliances. After the French forces under Napoleon invaded Egypt in 1798, they turned their eyes toward the Holy Land. Although the invaders easily captured Jaffa, Ramleh and Lydda, their siege of Acre failed. The fortifications of the city withstood the French onslaughts, and eventually the invaders returned to Egypt.

A volunteer introduces Ethiopian immigrants to Israeli foods and shopping customs.

An immigrant Ethiopian father and child.

A large group of Iranian Jews arrive in Israel in 1958.

By the eighteenth century the Hassidic movement, first launched by Rabbi Israel ben Eliezer, known as the Ba'al Shem Tov, had spread to the Holy Land from Ukraine and Russia. The Hassidim of that era settled in Tiberias and nearby Galilee villages; they were quickly followed by East European Jews who were adherents of the *Ga'on* of Vilna, and who fiercely opposed the tenets of the Hassidic teaching.

There were sporadic attempts by Christian missionary groups to set up schools and churches in the Holy Land; these efforts, mostly occurring in the eighteenth century, were met with limited success. By the middle of the same century virtually all of the western countries, including the United States, had formal consular offices in Jerusalem. Under Turkish rule, modernization of the country continued apace. By 1880 some 450,000 people resided in the Holy Land, of whom 24,000 were Jews and 45,000 were Christians.

During this period, the city of Jerusalem was the principal community in the country, with a population of 25,000. The historic Old City, divided into four quarters—Armenian, Christian, Moslem and Jewish—was now an enclave within an enlarged and expanding city.

In the mid-1800s the Jews of the Holy Land resided principally in the country's four cities holy to the Jews: Jerusalem, Hebron, Safed and Tiberias. They subsisted mainly on charity funds furnished by Jewish communities in the Diaspora. In 1831 historian J. Conder, describing the heavy tax burdens suffered by the Jews, wrote: "The extortions and suppressions were so numerous that it was said of the Jews they had to pay for the very air they breathed." Despite the hardships, Jewish immigration to the country continued throughout the 1800s. The introduction of a steamship route directly from Odessa, in southern Russia, to Jaffa eased the journey for many.

The first Hebrew printing press was set up in Safed in 1831; but, in 1837 an earthquake decimated the city, which never regained its leading role as a religious and cultural center of Judaism.

By the middle of the nineteenth century, plans for a Jewish state in the Holy Land that could serve as a buffer between Turkey and Egypt were put forth, but never materialized. For their own political goals and reasons, Britain and France extended limited protection to the Jews of the country during this period. Specific plans for the creation of a Jewish state were drawn up by both Jews and Christians, primarily in England, and won a measure of popular support. But these, too, came to naught.

In the country proper, Jews were fighting on another front: the missionaries were making inroads, especially with the poorest Jews, and the Turkish authorities were ignoring most efforts to stop them.

Conflicts also arose internally between the Sephardic Jews and their Ashkenzic coreligionists, often based on the former's claims to having been in the country longer than the newcomers.

A RETURN TO THE SOIL

Although it is difficult to pinpoint the exact date when modern Israel first began, many historians cite the year 1873, when the agricultural settlement Mikve Israel was established, offering courses in modern, scientific farming. The school-settlement, located in the center of the country, was set up with the assistance of the French-Jewish educational organization, Alliance Israelite Universelle.

An American consul living in Jerusalem in 1870 reported that some one thousand Jews in the Holy Land earned their livelihood as farmers and no longer as "paupers and beggars." Some historians note that the appearance of the first Hebrew-language publication in 1863, *Halevanon,* was the first step on the long, arduous journey back to an independent Jewish state after nearly two millennia of exile.

Realistically and historically, one can claim that it took nearly a full century for Israel to emerge in 1948. In the late 1800s, thoughtful Jews were deeply disappointed by the failure of the free world to solve the so-called Jewish question. In eastern Europe, notably in Czarist Russia, pogroms and restrictions against Jews continued unabated, often spurred by government officials.

In 1882 the political scientist Leon Pinsker, whose vocation was medicine, produced a short book titled *Autoemancipation* which stated flatly and unequivocally that the only solution to anti-Semitism was for the Jews to have a land of their own, where they could determine their own destiny and defend their citizens. The book appeared soon after a particularly brutal series of pogroms in and around the Russian city of Kishinev. Younger Jews reacted by forming the Hibat Zion (Love of Zion) movement, and by making plans to settle once again on the soil of the ancient Jewish homeland.

In 1894 a traumatic event took place in Paris that galvanized the embryonic first steps towards Jewish statehood: the trial and conviction, on trumped up charges of treason, of a French-Jewish officer. Alfred Dreyfus was sentenced to imprisonment on notorious Devil's Island, where he was incarcerated for five years. He was then returned to France, re-tried, found innocent and exonerated of all charges.

*Masada, a mountain site in Israel's south, where Jews fought hero-
ically against the Romans nearly two thousand years ago. Today
it is used for Bar Mitzvah boys from both Israel and abroad.
Shown, a Bar Mitvah ceremony, held under a wedding canopy.*

Israel's southern desert region, the Negev, comprises sixty percent of the country's territory. Large-scale programs have been launched to develop the area. Shown is a road in the Negev connecting two biblical cities, Beersheba and Sodom.

Despite the fact that Dreyfus was completely cleared, Parisian mobs roamed the streets, shouting "Death to the Jews!" Theodor Herzl, a young Jewish journalist and playwright stationed in the French capital for his prestigious Vienna newspaper, found himself profoundly affected by the trial and its aftermath—although he was at the time far from being a committed, observant Jew. In reaction to the Dreyfus affair he wrote a short book titled *The Jewish State* in which he insisted that the Jewish people's only future lay in creating an independent state of their own.

The Pinsker appeal for a Jewish homeland brought about a positive reaction mainly from intellectuals; the Herzl call, essentially for the same goal, caught the imagination of the Jewish masses, particularly in Poland, Rumania and Russia—all of whom were subjected to brutal attacks at the slightest provocation. In the more western countries, such as England, France and Germany, the reaction was cool; but, in the United States, which at the time had a dominant Jewish population made up of German-Jewish immigrants, the reaction was often hostile to Herzl and his new-fangled Zionist movement. Indeed, a leading Reform rabbi of the time, Bohemian-born Isaac Mayer Wise, in a well-publicized speech declared that the "new Zion is Cincinnati," where he had founded a Reform rabbinical seminary.

Herzl, whose appearance was striking and who was described by some as the "king of the Jews," set about to activate his ideas. In 1897 the first session of the World Zionist Congress took place in Switzerland, with delegates participating from around the world, including those from the small Jewish community in Palestine. A year later Herzl tried unsuccessfully to obtain support for a Jewish state from the German and Turkish heads of state, and then turned his attention instead to seeking support from Britain. Soon after, a bank to fund the movement was established, followed by the land-reclamation agency, the Jewish National Fund. When the British offered Herzl the territory of Uganda in eastern Africa as the site for a Jewish state, he was quick to accept, only to be defeated by delegates to the Zionist congress. They insisted that Jews must return to the ancient homeland, and nowhere else.

PRACTICAL FIRST STEPS

Herzl continued to seek support from high government officials, including those from Russia and Italy. When he died at the age of forty-four, he had been struggling to turn his dream into a reality for only nine years. But the spark that he ignited had caught on, and over the years the Zionist movement grew and enabled modern Israel to emerge. In one of his memoirs Herzl wrote that he was certain that the Jewish state would exist in fifty years. Ultimately, his prophecy was off by only five years.

At the beginning of the twentieth century the early Zionist leaders, men of intellect and pragmatism, cast their eyes on Turkish-controlled Palestine for many reasons: firstly, it was the ancient, divinely-promised Jewish homeland; secondly, the territory was sparsely inhabited by varied religious groups who lacked any semblance of national ambition; thirdly, the land itself, although dormant and weakened by centuries of neglect and misuse, was eminently suitable for renewal and restoration.

The early Zionist embers gradually caught fire. Although large masses of Jews from eastern Europe were emigrating to the United States, Canada, England and other destinations, young Jews, mostly students, sought to start their lives anew in the Holy Land: but, they wanted to do so not as charity recipients but as

A frontal view of Hadassah's Mt. Scopus Medical Center in Jerusalem.

Golda Meir, brought to the United States as a small child from Russia and raised in Milwaukee, became Israel's prime minister.

tillers of the soil, helping to reconstruct the ancient Jewish nation on its ancestral ground. These early Zionists also wanted to revive Hebrew, modernize it, and put an end to what they called Diaspora languages, such as Yiddish and Ladino. Simultaneously, they wanted to rid themselves of all trappings of the "ghetto personality." This, they interpreted as a persecuted minority living in a dominant, often bigoted majority. They were determined, they told each other and anyone who would listen, to be "a modern normal people."

The first pioneering efforts almost ended in disaster. The soil was infested with swamps and malaria; further, the young would-be farmers lacked experience as well as sufficient capital. At times they employed cheap Arab labor which they soon came to realize would defeat their own high ideals of working the land with their own hands. Fortunately, the Hibat Zion people, the philanthropic Baron Edmond de Rothschild, as well as the growing World Zionist Organization, came to the aid of the struggling pioneers.

BALFOUR DECLARATION ISSUED

A new wave of immigrants to Palestine began to arrive in 1905, from Russia and Poland, including David Ben Gurion, Yitzhak Ben Zvi and other embryonic leaders—all of whom were determined to build a genuine Jewish working class on the Land of Israel's ancient soil. Their goal was a society that would be productive and self-sufficient, and would in no way resemble their former Diaspora communities. Life during this time was extremely difficult, both economically and healthwise. Certainly, not all of the early pioneers persisted; many returned to their former homes, while others migrated to the new world of the western hemisphere.

Despite the great hardships, enough of the original settlers carried on and very slowly began to build a Hebrew-speaking, productive Jewish society. Those early years before the outbreak of World War I were also marked by initial efforts to create an underground self-defense organization, as well as some form of educational infrastructure for the future Jewish state. At the same time, the world Zionist movement strove to get its message across to millions of Jews in all corners of the world in order to advance its overall goals.

In 1917, during the First World War, Britain issued the Balfour Declaration, pledging support for the establishment of a "Jewish National Home" in Palestine. This was a momentous event; when the war ended a year later, large masses of Jews from eastern Europe immigrated to Palestine to become part of the expanding Jewish community.

The bulk of European Jewry at the time was to be found in Russia. After the Communist revolution and the installation of the Soviet regime, the Jews were not permitted to emigrate, nor to observe the tenets and customs of their faith. The Zionists now centered their attention on Jews in the Baltic states, Poland, Rumania and central Europe, urging them toward Palestine.

A widespread chain of mutual assistance organizations began to develop in the country among the growing Jewish population: *Histadrut,* a federation of trade unions, sought to assure workers of a decent standard of living; and the *kibbutzim* and *moshavim* (collectives and cooperatives) attracted growing numbers of immigrants. Their locations were carefully determined to form a network of defensible points in the Land of Israel, awaiting the day when the land would be transformed into a viable state.

A modern hospital laboratory in Jerusalem.

Contemporary Jerusalem is proud of its many parks, museums, hotels and Israeli government offices.

As the years passed, the native-born sons and daughters *(sabras)* became a distinctively different grouping within the country. Their native tongue, quite naturally, was Hebrew. They easily took to manual labor, especially on the soil, as though they had been farmers ages ago. They even seemed to gain confidence, to speak openly and without guile, and to exist in harmony with one another and with the country.

In the 1920s and 1930s, the Jewish community, which was governed by the British mandate, voluntarily donated taxes to its own local court system and nascent local and national government infrastructure. It did not take the Jews of Palestine long to realize that if they wished in time to attain an independent Jewish state, they would have no one to depend upon except themselves. They did hope and expect, however, that Jewish communities in the Diaspora would come forward with some financial backing.

The British regime—appointed by the League of Nations to govern Palestine after the end of World War I when the provinces of the former Ottoman empire were divided among the victorious Allies—was seen to be hostile to an independent state, principally because of vast quantities of oil being discovered in the area. The Arabs, with whom most Jews had hoped to have amicable relations as the conditions in Palestine improved and living standards elevated, were openly and violently opposed to the idea of a Jewish State. The rise of Nazism in Germany and Hitler's coming to power, coupled with the pro-Nazi stance of some Arab leaders, such as the Mufti of Jerusalem, convinced the Jews that the road ahead would be filled with obstacles. In order to succeed, they would have to become as independent as possible in providing arms for themselves.

A view of Tel Aviv across the Mediterranean from ancient Jaffa. In the early years of the twentieth century, Tel Aviv was a stretch of sand dunes; today it is Israel's largest metropolitan area.

Research programs in the Hadassah hospital labs are intensive and up to the highest western standards.

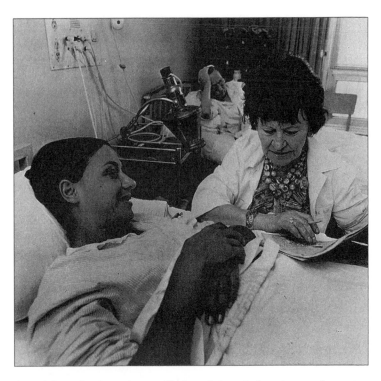

A social worker interviews a Hadassah hospital patient to determine the best treatment for her full recovery.

Like Jews in the United States and in other parts of the Diaspora, the Palestinian Jews were overwhelmed with grief when reports of the Holocaust began to filter out. For many Jews in Palestine, the Jewish Holocaust victims were close family members; yet, realistically, the leadership concluded that there was very little they could do to rescue their fellow Jews. Nevertheless, thousands of Jews volunteered and served with the British forces. At one point during the war, when the Nazi troops under Rommel were crossing North Africa on their way to Egypt, it looked as if they planned to attack Palestine. Contingency plans were prepared on how to resist and sustain the Jews. Fortunately, in the end, the British drove the Nazis back, never allowing them to reach Egypt or Palestine.

When World War II ended with the Germans' defeat, Jews and non-Jews throughout the world were crushed and traumatized by the extent of the Holocaust, which had resulted in the deliberate massacre of six million Jews. Between the war's end in 1945 and Israel's proclamation of statehood three years later, survivors of the Holocaust ignored British immigration restrictions to Palestine, and struggled against overwhelming odds to enter the country. Thousands succeeded, while thousands more were caught on the high seas and imprisoned on Cyprus for months and sometimes years at a time.

Now, in its first half-century of independence, Israel has increased its population tremendously. Empty areas of the country have been filled with towns, villages and farms, and agriculture and industry alike have been scientifically updated. Despite external threats, Israel's democracy has remained steadfast, standards of health and education have constantly been improved, antagonism between the Arab world and Israel has abated and two of its immediate neighbors, Egypt and Jordan, have signed peace treaties.

Israel faces challenges as the second half of its first century looms: how to balance secular Jewish values and strictly Orthodox traditions, and how to integrate recent immigrants, including close to 50,000 Ethiopian Jews and more than 900,000 Jews from the former Soviet Union, who are often unfamiliar with Jewish culture or are married to non-Jews.

And if the demographers are right, and two-thirds of the Jewish people make their homes in Israel within the next forty years or so, it is obvious that the need for more homes, food, jobs, and schools will continue to increase.

THE PRISM OF JEWISH HISTORY

To fully understand modern Israel—and especially its people who originate from scores of other countries and who brought with them dozens of other languages—it is necessary to become acquainted with the history of the Jewish people, beginning with Abraham, the biblical patriarch generally regarded as the first Jew. Most people are familiar with the biblical narrative of Abraham, his son Isaac, and Isaac's son, Jacob. The Bible relates the story of Jacob's twelve sons, from whom sprang twelve separate tribes. The Jews of today, those who reside in Israel as well as those who live outside, are all descended from only two tribes: Judah and Benjamin. The other ten tribes, who had formed a separate country in the ancient homeland, were captured in battle. They were either enslaved, exiled and scattered throughout the then known world, or killed. Nobody knows for sure; that is why they are called the Ten Lost Tribes.

Tel Aviv's state-of-the-art Dizengoff Center boasts a busy, multi-level interior mall with several hundred shops, restaurants and theaters.

Sidewalk cafés can be found in many of Israel's cities.

THE LONGEST EXILE

Until May 14, 1948, when Israel declared its statehood, Jews in all parts of the world, for long centuries, had ended their prayer services on Yom Kippur—the holiest and most awesome day of the Jewish calendar—with four words: "Next Year in Jerusalem!" The words were part of the concluding service, after which people generally rushed home to break their day-long fast. On the joyous holiday of Passover, when family and friends gather around the table at the annual Seder and read and sing the texts of the Haggadah booklet, they too conclude with the same four words: "Next Year in Jerusalem!" But it wasn't until Israel became an independent state again after two millennia of exile that people began to pay attention to the magical four words.

Until that time most Jews likely thought that in the far-off future, in messianic days, Israel would rise again. It was a nice way to end the service, certainly—but things changed radically after 1948. Dreams and hopes gave way to reality: a modern, full-fledged Jewish state now existed. The course of Jewish history had taken a sharp turn, and there was no going back.

As early as 1949, one man wrote that wherever he went it seemed to him that Jews were standing taller and straighter. Finally, having surmounted past hardships, a Jewish country had come into existence. Most Jews at the time, watching tens of thousands of Holocaust survivors and refugees from the Moslem world pour into the old-new Jewish homeland, came up with the same hindsight analysis: Had Israel been in existence in the 1930s and 1940s, how many hundreds of thousands of imperiled Jews, maybe even millions, could have been saved?

The new state in the Middle East meant that great changes would now be implemented in all aspects of Jewish life. Israel's Independence Day, called *Yom Ha'atzma'ut*, became a joyous, annual celebration, both for Jews in Israel and for those living in the Diaspora. Most synagogues in the western world, including the United States, which were accustomed to including a regular prayer for the well-being of the country and its leaders, now added an additional prayer for Israel's welfare.

The word "Israeli" slowly became a part of people's vocabulary. In the United States especially, Jews mounted successful campaigns to help the new state, perhaps assuaging feelings of guilt for not having done enough to rescue fellow Jews in Nazi-dominated Europe during the years of World War II.

In synagogues throughout the world, rabbinical sermons stressed the historic times the world was experiencing; perhaps, indeed, the long-awaited messianic era was on the horizon.

JEWS AND EXILE

Ironically and miraculously, from early times Jews have succeeded in maintaining their religious-national identity while at the same time holding onto their dream of returning to the homeland. One need only think of the biblical account of Jacob and his twelve sons, progenitors of the twelve tribes. No sooner had they begun to settle on the land when famine struck; they proceeded to Egypt where they were invited to stay and partake of the bountiful crops there. And not long after the whole community was enslaved, until Moses came and led them out of Egypt.

Despite the availability of modern supermarkets, Israelis enjoy shopping in the shuk, *the open-air markets that can be found all over the country. Pictured is the Machane Yehuda open-air market in Jerusalem.*

Finally, the Israelites attained their goal and settled down in their new homes, in a "land of milk and honey." For some three hundred years they lived in considerable peace, governed by judges—that is, until the Israeli people looked around them and noticed that all other peoples had a king, so they demanded one as well. The period of the kings began with Saul, the first Jewish king, who reigned for some twenty-five years. He was followed by the great King David, who sat on the throne for some forty years in Jerusalem and made it the capital. King David, in turn, was followed by his son Solomon, who built the Holy Temple and ruled for thirty-five years.

Life in the country was turbulent. Although there were relatively small wars in and around the country, for the most part people remained in their own homes, in their own homeland.

Then, around 925 B.C.E., the united kingdom of the Jewish state split: in the north ten tribes formed their own country, calling it Israel; in the south the two remaining tribes, Judah and Benjamin, also established a new state and named it Judea. Two centuries later the Assyrians conquered Israel, and from that time on the world has never really resolved the riddle of the Lost Tribes. (All Jews in the world today, both Ashkenazic and Sephardic, are descended from Judea.)

Two hundred years after the Assyrians had defeated and captured the people of (northern) Israel, another warring country, Babylon, conquered (southern) Judea, and its people were shipped to Babylon (today's Iraq).

The exile in Babylon was relatively short, and after fifty years the Jews were allowed to return home. The Persian empire, which had trounced the Assyrians, helped the Jews return to Judea. Almost as soon as the Jews returned to Jerusalem, they began work on the second Holy Temple.

For about a century, peace reigned in Judea; worship and religious study, led by Ezra the Scribe, were focused in Jerusalem. Ezra and Nehemiah were determined to improve the terrible economic and social conditions pervading Judea.

On the European continent, a new force arose: Alexander the Great. Originally from Macedon in northern Greece, he conquered the Persian empire which then included Judea. Soon after his death, Alexander's generals set up separate kingdoms in Egypt and Syria, and each fought for control of Judea in the south and Israel in the north. Meanwhile, Hellenism began to dominate the culture of the world. For the first time, the Bible was translated into Greek, which was then the dominant language of the region. For Jews, the new state of affairs posed a serious dilemma: they realized both the benefits and dangers for the Jewish religion and for Jewish people should this foreign influence, known as Hellenism, gain the upper hand. Nevertheless, many Jews chose to live in a new Diaspora, primarily in Alexandria, Egypt, the coastal cities of Greece, and along the Mediterranean—presumably for economic rewards.

This was the first time that Jews opted to leave their homes and self-exile themselves. They likely prospered initially, but in the large Egyptian port city of Alexandria, the Jews became Hellenized, spoke Greek and assimilated. Nonetheless, when they sought to obtain citizenship a few centuries later, it was denied them. Anti-Jewish riots broke out in the first century of the common era; in the fifth century, all of Alexandria's Jews were expelled.

About a century after Alexander's forces simultaneously defeated the Persians and the Jews, Antiochus, a Syrian Seleucid leader, conquered the Jewish homeland. He strove to do away with Judaism, substituting it with the prevailing Hellenistic way of life. His efforts led to a revolt by the Hasmonean family,

*A Haredi, an ultra-Orthodox Jew, shown with his son as they proceed
to the synagogue on Sabbath in Jerusalem's ancient Old City.*

whose five sons were known as the *Maccabees* (hammerers). The Maccabees' success in preventing the abolition of Judaic rituals is celebrated today in the annual Hanukkah festival. The Maccabees' chief success was the cleansing of the Holy Temple, and its rededication as a main center of Jewish worship.

In 140 B.C.E., Judea had become a viable, independent state despite the fact that many Judeans had chosen to live in self-exile. Under the Maccabee influence the country prospered and bolstered its religious-national aims.

HEROD SEIZES THE THRONE

This situation was not to last however. Herod, a tyrannical usurper, seized the Judean throne in 37 B.C.E. with the help of the Romans. Herod proclaimed himself king of the Jews. Although considered despotic and vicious, he managed to expand the small state's borders, improve economic conditions, enlarge the Temple in Jerusalem, and build cities and fortresses throughout the country. He extended his political and economic protection to the Jews in the Diaspora.

At Herod's death, the Jewish kingdom that he had ruled with an iron hand did not survive. Judea became a province of the Roman empire. By the conclusion of the first century C.E., Jews lived in almost every corner of the vast Roman empire; they comprised about ten percent of the overall population. At the time, nearly half of the world's Jews resided in Judea, and half in the Roman empire—especially in Egypt, Greece, Syria and Rome. Jews in the Roman Diaspora enjoyed religious freedom during this era. Large numbers also resided in Babylon and its environs. Most historians believe that the Jewish people's dispersion actually bolstered them; their fellow Jews in Judea were expelled by the Romans soon after the destruction of the Holy Temple, an act that followed the failed Jewish revolt against the Romans in Judea.

One ancient historian, Josephus, estimated that the number of Jews then living in the Roman empire totaled some seven million people; he voiced the opinion that this impressive figure had resulted naturally from both increasing births and from sizable numbers of converts to Judaism.

During this period the Jewish dispersion reached westward to what is today France and Spain, and eastward to various countries along the Tigris River. Unlike many other dispersed people, the Jews of this period succeeded in retaining their traditions and religious practices and thus their overall unique identity. This characteristic would accompany them in the coming centuries as their earlier dispersion became a Diaspora that would continue for some two thousand years.

Over the course of the new millennium, a new religion—Christianity—took shape and spread rapidly. The Jews in their ancient homeland suffered expulsion, and the economic and political condition of their compatriots in the various lands in which they were dispersed suffered major declines in their status. In the seventh century, the Persians took control of the Holy Land, and for about a decade allowed the Jews to rule themselves; but soon after, Arabs from the surrounding countries—most of whom had by now converted to the new Islamic religion—seized Jerusalem. They dominated the Holy Land for four centuries, until the Turkish Seljuks defeated them. At the start of the new millennium, the Crusaders arrived; and, for the next ten centuries, control of the country wavered between the

Arabs, Turks, Crusaders, and after the First World War, even the British. Since 1948, following a decision of the United Nations, the state of Israel has risen on roughly three-quarters of the western part of ancient Palestine assigned to the Jewish state; Jordan, established in 1922, occupies the much larger region east of the Jordan River.

THE TALMUD

During this bleak period of Jewish exile, there was one bright spot: the ancient Jewish community of Babylon, in existence since the sixth century B.C.E. Cognizant of the destruction of the Temple in Jerusalem and wishing to ensure the continuity of Jews and Judaism, the Babylon community placed great emphasis on Torah study and local synagogue worship. The synagogues set up in each area became centers of worship, study and assembly, while the new, profound study of the Torah—the first Five Books of the Hebrew Bible—developed new generations of scholars, and kept the Jews' appreciation of their religious heritage alive.

Over a period of centuries, the commentaries, analyses and explanations of every syllable in the Torah by the best of rabbis and scholars were collected and preserved; by the sixth century C.E., the Babylonian Talmud was completed. It remains to this day a remarkable source of Jewish teaching and is accepted as the Oral Law, virtually on the same footing as the Torah itself which dates back to Moses and Mount Sinai.

The Talmudic texts, dealing with every aspect of daily life and with issues confronting the Jewish community were, and remain, of inestimable value in assuring the viability and vibrancy of Jewish life. The scholars, whose deliberations as well as rulings are included in the Talmud, enabled schools of Jewish study to be established all over the world and provided them with textual material that requires many years, if not a lifetime, to master. A similar Talmudic text, known as the Jerusalem Talmud, was created in the Holy Land; however, by universal agreement, the Babylonian Talmud is regarded as by far the more significant.

From the eighth to the thirteenth centuries, most of the world's Jewish population lived under Moslem rule. By and large they enjoyed freedom and prosperity, even though they were regarded as second-class citizens. Jews had to walk in the gutter if a Moslem walked on the sidewalk, in most Moslem lands. The political leaders of the countries in which the Jews lived generally encouraged them to leave their farming endeavors and move to urban areas to help develop trading and mercantile establishments. The Jews were strongly influenced by Arabic culture, and Arabic soon became their primary language. Beginning around the thirteenth century, the Jews gradually migrated to the European continent, where the countries and populations were principally Christian. By the middle of the 1600s, half of the world's Jews lived in Moslem lands, and half in Christian countries.

The Jewish community of Italy can trace its roots back some 1,900 years and at times it was the third largest Jewish population in Europe. Jews made a living as dyers, weavers and traders; a number of Talmudic academies opened in Rome, Lucca and Ottranto. Although protected by papal decree from coerced conversions, the Jews' legal rights were sharply limited.

When the Inquisition in Spain began in the fifteenth century, its influence spread to southern Italy; in the north, however, Jews prospered as bankers. After movable type was invented in 1455, the Italian Jews were the first to implement it for the printing of Hebrew books.

Jews had lived in Spain from the third century until the expulsion by the Catholic Church's Inquisition in 1492. Historical records show that Spain was divided between Christians and Moslems. Most historians have concluded that under Christian rule in Spain, the Jews were treated barbarously, while the Moslems were tolerant of them. The so-called Golden Age of the Jews of Spain, when they prospered economically and produced memorable literary and scholarly works, took place under the Moslems; this was analogous to the heights of Jewish communal history attained in Babylon and, later, in Poland.

One of the many outstanding Spanish-Jewish personalities of that period was Judah Halevi, a physician, poet and philosopher whose works are still a vital part of contemporary Jewish study. He was also, in the twelfth century, an early Zionist, regarding the incessant battles between Christians and Moslems in Spain as a foreign venue for Jews. In his *Poems of Zion* and other works, he wrote that there is no physical security for Jews anywhere but in the ancestral homeland—that this is the only place where Jews can fully realize their spiritual potential.

One of the greatest Jewish personalities of the two-thousand-year exile was Maimonides, who lived from 1135-1204. His full Hebrew name was Rabbi Moses ben Maimon, and the other name by which he is known, Rambam, is an acronym for his Hebrew name. He produced two major works, though either one of them would have sufficed to establish him as an intellectual and religious giant in the annals of the Jewish people. His code of Jewish law, *Mishneh Torah,* and his *Guide for the Perplexed,* are studied in Jewish schools and religious seminaries to this day. He was also a physician and medical researcher.

At the age of thirteen, Maimonides' family left Spain because of Moslem fundamentalist persecution and wandered throughout North Africa, finally settling in Egypt. Eventually he devoted his time to his medical practice, his religious scholarship, and his responsibilities as a communal Jewish leader. One of his most popular works is his "Thirteen Principles of Faith," an attempt to concisely summarize the teachings and beliefs of Judaism. When Jews in Nazi death camps were marched to the crematoria, they sang his words, expressing hope and belief in God and in the future.

PUBLIC RELIGIOUS DEBATES

Over a period of centuries, Spain's Jewish community produced great rabbis, scholars, physicians and other men of intellect, but also continued to search for the significance of the Jewish people's long exile within the parameters of religious experience. Rabbis, in Spain and France, too, found themselves compelled to carry out public theological disputes with church leaders.

In 1263, one such disputation took place in Spain. Nahmanides—like Maimonides, a physician and religious commentator—was arrayed against a group of church officials in a widely-publicized public debate in Barcelona. A brilliant speaker and highly knowledgeable, Nahmanides won the public confrontation, but only to be exiled soon after. Thenceforth, church leaders intensified their efforts to convert Jews, and increased public burnings of Talmudic and other Jewish religious texts.

During this same period, a new phenomenon appeared in Jewish life: a profound effort to understand God's attitude toward the Jewish people inasmuch as their suffering continued unabated. This new development was designated as *Kabbalah,* or Jewish mysticism. The new philosophy's basic text, the *Zohar,* appeared in the last years of the thirteenth century. Many rabbis cautioned against studying it, at least until one reached the age of forty and had already spent many years mastering the Bible and Talmud.

Meanwhile, in England, where Jews had lived since the eleventh century, conditions were deteriorating as Richard the Lionhearted assumed the throne in 1189. Formerly, Jews had prospered, and now their property and possessions were gradually being confiscated; by the end of the thirteenth century, and after being impoverished, the Jews were expelled from the country. Prior to the brutal expulsion decree, massacres of Jewish communities were carried out, notably in York.

The church's fervor in spreading its doctrines continued to intensify, especially in Spain where it was determined that everyone in the country, without exception, was to become Catholic. Many Jews avoided being expelled by overtly converting, but covertly continuing to observe Jewish religious laws and customs. They came to be known as *Marranos* or *Conversos;* in many cases, despite their conversion, they continued to be cruelly oppressed. These persecutions reached a climax in 1492, when all Jews in Spain were expelled.

The Inquisition, as the church program came to be called, followed those Jews seeking refuge in the newly-discovered lands of Latin America. Some Jews, fearing the church's wrath and the very real threat of public executions of non-Catholics, migrated in the 1500s and 1600s from Brazil and Mexico northward to safety in territories that eventually became the southwestern regions of the United States.

In the middle of Europe, in what in time became Germany, Jews from the tenth century onwards at first prospered. Barred from joining the guilds or earning their livelihoods by farming, the exiles became traders and money lenders. In the thirteenth and fourteenth centuries, widespread attacks on Jews took place in Germany, resulting in the massacre of hundreds of thousands. Somehow they managed to survive, and many remained in the country. However, in the fifteenth and sixteenth centuries Jews from Germany, attracted by a greater sense of tolerance as well as by economic opportunities, began to settle in the east, particularly in Poland and Lithuania.

The development of modern printing at this time was an enormous stimulus to all educational and religious groups; Hebrew printing, in fact, grew at a faster pace than general, secular printing, apparently because Jews recognized it as a modern marvel that would help to ensure Jewish learning and continuity. At first, Hebrew printing presses were centered in Italy, then later moved to Amsterdam. In time, virtually every major Jewish community had its own Hebrew typesetting and printing tradition.

By the fifteenth century, Protestant groupings within Christianity had developed; Jews hoped and believed that this would lead to a more tolerant and embracing environment for them. Amsterdam, during this period, became a commercial and intellectual center for European Jews, many of whom had found refuge there after fleeing the Inquisition. Many were also *Marranos*, who now resumed their Jewish identity openly.

In the New World (the western hemisphere) a momentous event took place in 1654. A group of Jewish refugees—four men, six women and thirteen children—arrived at New Amsterdam seeking haven and a new life. They had escaped from Brazil, fearful that the far-reaching Inquisition would harm them. The governor of the city (that would eventually change its name to New York), Peter Stuyvesant, wanted to send them away; he believed Jews to be "Christ blasphemers." But his employers, the Dutch West India Company, thought otherwise. Ultimately, the Jews were allowed to remain, travel and work; they could even have a burial ground, but no synagogue. From that tiny beginning, the American Jewish community took root in the United States, numbering some six million. Over the years, the Jews of America have made vital, substantial contributions to the country.

A few years earlier in 1648, and across the world in Ukraine, large numbers of Jews were living under rigid Czarist conditions. During this time, a Cossack nationalist named Bogdan Chmielnicki—ostensibly seeking to rid the Ukrainian area of Polish domination—launched a series of attacks against the Jews. The pogroms, which lasted for two full years, resulted in the massacres of tens of thousands of Jews, most of them poor, religious farmers living in modest villages and those employed as managers of large Polish estates. Until the rise of Hitler in Germany, no single enemy of the Jewish people had murdered as many and as ruthlessly as Chmielnicki and his Cossack bands.

The Ukrainian disaster laid the groundwork for the Jews' deep sense of hopelessness and depression. It also encouraged masses of Jews to believe that the true Messiah was at hand, and would lead them back to the Holy Land and a vastly different life; for, traditionally, it is believed that the advent of the Messiah would follow a time of horrific catastrophes. The Jews therefore believed that the massacres in Ukraine meant that they would soon be redeemed. In 1665 a feverish atmosphere seized the Jews when they heard that Shabbetai Zevi, a Turkish Jew, had acknowledged that he was indeed the long-awaited Messiah.

Most historians agree that Shabbetai Zevi was a manic depressive. He was expelled from his home community in Turkey for flagrant violations of religious law. Word that this strange young man was the true Messiah spread like wildfire throughout eastern Europe. Everywhere, Jews prayed, fasted and some even flagellated themselves in order to hasten the day of redemption. Many Jews sold their belongings and left at once for the ancestral homeland, confident that messianic days were on the horizon.

But in 1666, when Zevi set foot on Turkish soil, he was arrested. His sentence: convert to Islam, or be executed. Zevi converted, and a few hundred followers joined him; but, for the bulk of Jews around the world, his conversion was a source of disbelief, shock and sorrow. The entire episode traumatized Jews for many decades.

In the eighteenth century, in response to a life of poverty, hopelessness and fear of pogroms, thousands of Jews in Poland and Ukraine, and later all over the world, joined a new movement: Hassidism. In a way, this fast-growing movement was also a reaction to the previous century's murderous pogroms. It was a movement for the masses emphasizing prayer with song, joy in every aspect of life, and a diminution of excessive learning. Many rabbis and scholars opposed the Hassidim fiercely: but, the movement caught on, and even today remains a vibrant component of the Jewish community in the United States, Israel and in many other countries.

In the eighteenth and nineteenth centuries, the enlightenment era and the emancipation period ensued. The Jewish religion came to have new interpretations: Reform and Conservative, as well as Orthodox. The idealistic socialist ideas also attracted large numbers of Jews, who turned away from their religion, but in most cases not from Jewish—especially Yiddish—culture. The murderous pogroms in Czarist Russia in the last years of the nineteenth and the early part of the twentieth centuries spurred millions of Jews to abandon their homes in Russia, Poland and Rumania and reestablish themselves in the western world, particularly in the United States. And, as noted earlier, the modern political Zionist movement launched at the end of the nineteenth century culminated in the establishment of Israel, and the return of Jews to their ancient homeland.

ISRAEL IN THE NEW MILLENNIUM

David Ben Gurion, Israel's first prime minister, used to quip about his country: "You can't be a realist if you don't believe in miracles."

If Israel is anything, it is a land of miracles and paradoxes, where the unexpected frequently happens. Russian Jewry, for example, a vast reservoir of manpower and potential population, was truncated from the world Jewish community when the Soviet revolution took over the government.

Since that time, roughly seventy years from the Communist revolution until the Soviet collapse in the 1990s, it was generally believed that virtually all Russian Jews had been lost. After all, for some seven decades Bible study, the Hebrew language, and any Jewish rituals or traditions had been strictly prohibited.

And then the miracle began; a trickle of Russian Jews began to move out and resettle in Israel in the early 1970s. The trickle soon became a floodtide. Today the Jewish population of Israel is nearly twenty percent Russian (i.e. former residents of the Soviet Union), Ukraine, the Baltic area, Uzbekistan, Georgia and additional regions. These new immigrants—nearly a million strong—are learning the basics of Judaism; spouses are often converting to Judaism; children are growing up free and unafraid. A large number of these newcomers are scientists and engineers, and their presence in Israel has helped the country reach new heights of technological advancement.

In the early, formative years of the state, life in Israel was hard. Food was rationed, people subsisted on imported frozen food products, and the Arab boycott led to difficulties in establishing viable industries. Yet, somehow, miraculously, it all worked out. The young nation's democratic traditions remained intact; cultural endeavors expanded; housing, farms, factories, schools, and hospitals were all provided; the economy developed, providing genuine sustenance for the growing population.

The resurrection of the Hebrew language—the language of the Bible—which for two millennia of exile had been relegated to prayer and study and its transformation into a living tongue that united all segments of the population, was another miracle. When the Jews came to live in Israel during the last century, those who arrived as haven seekers and those who came out of ideological fervor, many of the trappings of their former lives in the long exile were discarded. This included the languages that had developed in their respective countries of origin—Yiddish, Ladino, Judeo-Arabic, and others. Modern Hebrew, whose vocabulary was expanded on almost a daily basis, became a vital, unifying force.

*A rare sight in Jerusalem today: an Arab on his camel, atop historic
Mount of Olives, with the modern city in the background.*

One of the many problems confronting Israel's planners and leaders is the country's lack of water. More population means more water is needed and consumed; various industries as well as modern, scientifically-planned agriculture require ever-growing water supplies. In the north, in Upper Galilee, the average annual rainfall totals some sixty inches; but, in the extreme south it measures less than one inch. To ease this situation, Israel developed a type of computerized irrigation called drip irrigation, assuring adequate supplies for crops while conserving the amount of water dispensed. This method has been taught by Israelis to farmers around the world who live in arid areas.

A millionaire was once quoted giving advice to an ambitious youngster: "Find a need and fill it." In a sense, this has been one of Israel's guiding principles. In 1909, when Jews made their way to Palestine from pogrom-ridden Russia, they felt the need for a city to be constructed on the shore of the Mediterranean, adjacent to the ancient biblical city of Jaffa. It did not take them long to turn this need into a reality, and there soon arose the city of Tel Aviv ("Hill of Spring"). Today, with its suburb, Tel Aviv is Israel's major metropolitan area and its commercial and cultural center.

Meanwhile, other settlers felt the strong need for the erection of agricultural collectives, known in Hebrew as *kibbutzim.* Here the workers pooled their efforts, laboring for the settlement and not for themselves, thus assuring that every kibbutz member and his family would be provided for. Although there have been modifications to this way of life, the system has proven to be a strong, dependable bulwark in Israel's development.

Non-Jewish visitors to Israel are sometimes at a loss to understand the strong emotional bond that links Jews in all parts of the world to this ancient and now reborn homeland. These visitors ask: "Why do you feel the need for a Jewish

Judaism's holiest site in Israel is the kotel, the Western Wall of the Holy Temple in Jerusalem. It is usually crowded with worshipers and tourists.

state? After all, you are citizens of America, England, France, etc. You have your own religion—isn't that enough?"

But, it is not. Most Jews, including those who express their innermost feelings and those who hide them, sense that no matter how much time has passed, the ugly phenomenon of anti-Semitism is never completely extinguished. Whatever the cause, anti-Semitism can only be seen as irrational, both in the eyes of the Jews and in those of thoughtful, rational Gentiles.

Many Jewish visitors to Israel often express the same awareness after being in the country a short time: "I feel more at ease here. I never knew, back home, that I always seemed to carry a psychological burden on my shoulders. I guess I always was a little apprehensive, maybe even fearful, of being in the minority in a primarily Christian country."

Some Jews express their fears differently: "Israel, for me, is an insurance policy. God forbid, if ever another Hitler should come to power, then I know I have a safe haven in Israel." One Jewish American multi-millionaire on a visit to Israel, met some distant relatives and announced his plans to buy an apartment in Jerusalem. His Israeli relations, aware of his luxurious homes in America, expressed surprise. To which he responded wistfully: "You never know, you never know."

Or, as the actor-comedian Alan King once put it: "America is my beloved wife, but Israel is my beloved mother."

Most Jews around the world have not fully recovered from the traumatic Six Day War of June 1967. For a time it looked like the massacre of European Jewry was to be repeated; Egypt, Syria and Jordan openly prepared for an all-out assault to drive the Jews into the sea. They were heavily armed by the Soviets. The bottom line quickly became clear: not one western democracy would come to Israel's rescue. Jews worldwide were momentarily traumatized, worrying about the Jews of Israel.

The miracle that took place, when the Israelis defeated the would-be attackers in a matter of hours and days, caused the Jews to breathe a deep sigh of relief and gratitude—and to realize how deeply they were committed to the Jewish homeland.

CULTURAL ATTAINMENTS

A recent report by the United Nations' UNESCO agency noted that per capita, the people of Israel are the world's biggest book readers. Many works—fiction, juvenile and general non-fiction—are produced in Hebrew; to date, Israel has achieved one Nobel Laureate in literature, S.Y. Agnon. Simultaneously, a large number of titles—scientific, technical, medical, fiction, juvenile—are adapted from various languages and published in Hebrew.

The elementary and high schools of the country are filled to capacity; education is compulsory up to age sixteen. Vocational and technical schools are training future technicians. University enrollment has surpassed 60,000, and a constant effort is being made to encourage teenagers from the poorer strata of society to obtain a higher education. Many Arab students, including those who reside in nearby Palestinian areas, are enrolled in medical and nursing schools in Israel.

Theater, motion pictures, concerts, television (including cable television) are all thriving. Many plays are originals, while others are Hebrew-language versions of works by Arthur Miller, Neil Simon and others. Israel's film industry is still new, but it has been progressing steadily; most movies shown today are American, with Hebrew subtitles. Due in part to the arrival of Russian newcomers, the number of orchestras in the country has

King George Street in downtown Jerusalem is a busy thoroughfare.

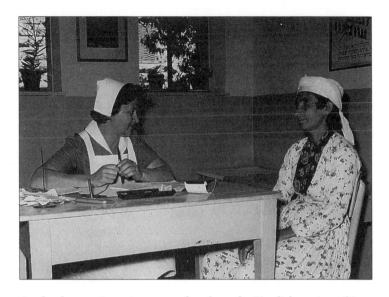

A school nurse interviews a mother from the Kurdish region of Iraq regarding professional guidance for her son.

expanded, and concerts in large and small cities alike are available almost nightly. Many television programs—which can be picked up in neighboring Arab countries—are designed to appeal to a diverse audience. Cable television in Israel is unusually varied, since many shows are European or American in origin.

The number of daily and weekly newspapers, in Hebrew and in practically every modern language, is staggering. In addition, there are two daily English-language newspapers, and many magazines in English in specialized fields.

Like their peers in western democracies, Israelis pursue sports with a passion, especially soccer (called football), basketball and tennis. When the Olympics come around every four years, Israelis keep hoping that an Israeli will win a gold medal, or at least a silver. It hasn't happened yet, although Israelis have been awarded less prestigious Olympic awards.

There is another passion in Israel—almost an obsession—that is unique to the country's Jewish population: archaeology. Young and old vie for an opportunity to dig in the truly ancient soil, and to bring up relics and remnants of the civilizations that existed in the same areas so many years ago.

It is not unusual to visit an Israeli friend's home where he or she will proudly display a mosaic excavated from a remote corner of the country. This obsession with archaeology has also caused serious clashes with some ultra-Orthodox Jews, who believe that ancient cemeteries should not be disturbed. Often the ancient cemeteries cannot be seen; but, those who object to the digging insist they know that they are there, and that is enough for the ultra-Orthodox to raise objections.

The Dead Sea Scrolls, which were found accidentally by a young Arab shepherd near the Dead Sea, caused a universal sensation when they were first brought to light some forty years ago. Leading scholars, both Jewish and Christian, spent many years interpreting the obsolete Hebrew characters, which eventually confirmed the identical text used today for biblical books. A permanent exhibition of the Scrolls is displayed in Jerusalem, alongside the Israel Museum.

Jerusalem, as might be expected, is filled with museums, housing both ancient and modern exhibits. Since the whole city, including the ancient Old City, came under Israeli control in the aftermath of the 1967 Six Day War, there has been total freedom of religion for all groups. The ancient Old City, divided into four quarters—Christian, Moslem, Armenian, and Jewish—is an unforgettable tourist site. Visits to the Hebrew University, the Knesset (parliament), the Supreme Court building, and the various medical centers maintained mostly by American Jews— these too should not be missed. Just outside the city's borders a beautiful forest has been planted, in memory of President John F. Kennedy, which is well worth a visit.

People often say that Israel has everything. One unique thing Jerusalem has is a beautiful new zoological garden, featuring nearly every creature mentioned in the Bible. Many of these animals were assembled from various parts of the world, having become extinct in Israel proper in the last two millennia.

The one place in Jerusalem that should not be missed is the Yad Vashem Holocaust memorial recalling the six million European Jews slaughtered by the Nazis. As one walks around this memorial and sees people from literally every corner of the world speaking in hushed tones in their respective languages, the horror that took place a half-century ago becomes all too real—especially, when one remembers that among the six million victims were one and a half million children.

ISRAEL'S PRECIOUS CHILDREN

Israelis seem to have a special attitude toward children; perhaps this is because so many were lost in the Holocaust. When a young soldier is lost on the battlefield, it seems that everybody, not just his family and friends, mourns. There is a cooperative spirit in Israel, especially when it comes to children.

People care and remember. This nationwide compassion expresses itself in many ways. Struggling parents will quickly find individuals volunteering to tutor and take care of their children. In apartment houses, doors often are kept unlocked so that needy children will know they have a place to go to for a meal or for emotional support.

There are, of course, many poor people in Israel; mostly they are newcomers struggling to find their place in the country. For children of nursery school age and for teens who require special help in their studies or motivational plans, there are dedicated volunteer support groups in the United States and in other democratic countries. These volunteers—many of them Jewish women—raise monetary funds and provide teachers, schools, and supplies, in addition to government-sponsored schools and supplementary support programs.

With few exceptions, every able-bodied Jewish eighteen-year-old, man or woman, must serve in the armed forces; after they are discharged, the men can be called for reserve duty up to the age of forty-five. For many teens from disadvantaged homes, military experience is a salutary period. By and large, Israeli Arabs are excused from service; the small Druze and Bedouin communities have always insisted on serving, and they continue to distinguish themselves in military service.

Na'amat's day care centers enable working mothers to drop off their children on their way to work.

A day care center where Israeli, Ethiopian and Russian children play together.

RELIGION IN ISRAEL

For the religious Jews, and certainly for the ultra-Orthodox known as *Haredim,* religion is a vital component of their lives, from birth to death. Some twenty-five percent of the Jewish community calls itself traditional, religious or ultra-Orthodox. Usually they are educated in their own schools (yeshivas); in the case of the Haredim, students continue their religious studies well in to their twenties.

The rest of the Jewish population is either entirely non-observant, or else they observe a modicum of Jewish tradition, such as Sabbath eve family dinner with lit candles on the table. Usually they choose to celebrate the festivals of Hanukkah, Jewish Arbor Day, Purim, Passover, Shavuot and Sukkot as national celebrations, and they participate fully. Of course they also celebrate Israel's Independence Day, as well as join in the somber observance of Holocaust Memorial Day and a special day paying tribute to Israel's fallen soldiers.

Although public schools in Israel do not teach religion per se, every student studies the Bible. Religious Jews in Israel— most of whom are Orthodox, with a far smaller sprinkling of Conservatives and Reforms—attend synagogue services daily; on Friday evenings and Saturday mornings, the synagogues are crowded with worshipers.

Generally the streets of Israel, on Saturday mornings and afternoons, are still. Few cars or buses are on the road, especially in Jerusalem. During this time, young secular Jews are often on the beach, which fills up early. Restaurants, particularly in Tel Aviv and Haifa, are open; retail shops, banks, post office branches, and most theaters and movie houses are closed. When dusk arrives, the streets come alive with traffic and the

The Mosque of Omar is Islam's holiest site in Jerusalem, one of the four holy cities of Islam. The dome at right is a Jerusalem landmark; it is covered in gold leaf.

sidewalks fill up with pedestrians, many of whom likely spent the afternoon napping or visiting.

Some of the rigidly religious Israelis have no contact with, or use for, irreligious Israelis. This same attitude prevails among the extremely secular vis-a-vis the religious elements. Most Israelis, it is safe to say, fall somewhere in between. When they marry, even the irreligious must use the services of an Orthodox rabbi; the alternative is to leave the country and have a civil wedding. Once married abroad, the Israeli law states that you are married. But in order to be married in Israel proper, Jews must apply to an Orthodox rabbi. The Orthodox rabbinate in Israel holds sway over all affairs of personal life. This monopoly, however, is slowly being challenged by the other branches of Judaism, as well as by the secular Jews.

Throughout the last two thousand years, Jews at synagogue service made sure they faced east when they prayed, toward Jerusalem. Jews in the Far East faced west, in the direction of Jerusalem. In Israel the feeling seems to be that Jerusalem pervades everything in the country, so this tradition is generally omitted.

Religious (male) Israeli soldiers are easily discernible by the skullcap (*yarmulke* or *kippa*) they wear at all times, in marked contrast to the military uniform and weapon they carry with them always; the soldiers divide their time between study and traditional military training.

ISRAEL'S MINORITIES

Israel's minorities are mainly Arab Moslems and also include Christians, Druzes, and Bedouins. They constitute roughly twenty percent of the country's population. The Arabs of Israel in 1948 totaled about 150,000; today they number nearly a million. The Arabic language is an official language, alongside Hebrew (street signs appear in both languages). There have always been Arab and Druze members of the Knesset, whose speeches are translated simultaneously.

Every effort is made to retain and bolster the Arabs' cultural and educational undertakings. Literacy among the Israeli Arabs is estimated at ninety-five percent, a remarkably higher number than in most Arab countries. There are a score of Arab-language periodicals; Arabic is taught in the Jewish high schools. More than five thousand Arabs are enrolled in Israel's universities and technical schools.

There are some 300,000 Arab children in Israel who study in nearly one thousand schools. All religious faiths are free to practice their religious traditions, and this law is fully enforced by the government. Each community has its own leaders and enjoys jurisdiction over its own practice. Israel's laws apply equally to all. All women in Israel have the right to vote; all girls as well as boys must be educated. Polygamy and child marriage are forbidden. The health facilities open to Jews are available on an equal basis to all minority groups.

It is interesting to recall that when Israel was proclaimed in May 1948 there were some 900,000 Jews living in Arab countries, many of them tracing their roots there as far back as two thousand years. After Israel was established, and after the defeat of the Arab countries, Jews in these lands felt obligated to leave. Most of them came to Israel. Today the number of Jews in Arab countries is less than 25,000.

Many Arab countries, including Saudi Arabia, Qatar, Bahrein, and others, deny entry visa to all Jews—not only to residents, but to tourists as well.

THE BUILDING OF A NATION

Most Americans know that the United States emerged when the early British colonies located on the Atlantic seaboard revolted against the British empire which then—in the late 1700s—was the leading political power in the world. The revolution came about largely for economic reasons, as well as the colonists' innate desire to govern themselves.

After the successful revolution against the crown, the Americans wisely set about to write a constitution that would lay out the new country's hopes and aspirations, and outline the full civil and human rights of its citizens. In the ensuing years, as the United States developed and its populace grew, large numbers of people migrated there from various European areas in search of religious and political freedom.

Israel's birth was radically different; although many of its new people also came in search of freedom, there was an even stronger motivation that precipitated the rebirth of the old-new homeland. Put simply, for some two thousand years, in virtually every corner of the world, Jews had been hounded, massacred, expelled—and basically they did not know why. Jews regarded themselves as decent, law-abiding people desiring a normal life. Even after the period of emancipation swept Europe, and life for many people improved greatly, contempt for Jews culminating in murderous anti-Semitism never seemed to cease. Jews continued to seek an answer to their question: *Why?*

One Polish Jew, Leon Pinsker, a physician who had contact with the non-Jewish community as well as with his coreligionists, also contemplated this problem. In 1882 he published a short book entitled *Autoemancipation* in which he tried to analyze the social and psychological roots of anti-Semitism. He wrote:

Among the living nations of the earth, the Jews occupy the position of a nation long since dead. With the loss of their homeland, the Jews lost their independence and fell into a state of decay which is incompatible with the existence of a whole and vital organism. The state was crushed by the Roman conquerors and vanished from the world's view. But after the Jewish people had yielded up its existence as an actual state, as a political entity, it could nevertheless not submit to total destruction—it did not cease to exist as a spiritual nation.

Thus, the world saw in this people the frightening form of one of the dead walking among the living. This ghost-like apparition of a people without unity or organization, without land or other bond of union, no longer alive, and yet moving among the living—this eerie form scarcely paralleled in history, unlike anything that preceded it or followed it, could not fail to make a strange impression upon the imagination of the nations.

And if the fear of ghosts is something inborn, and has a certain justification in the psychic life of humanity, is it any wonder that it asserted itself powerfully at the sight of this dead and yet living nation?

Fear of the Jewish ghost has been handed down and strengthened for generations and centuries. It led to a prejudice which paved the way for Judeophobia.

Along with a number of other subconscious and superstitious ideas, instincts and idiosyncrasies, Judeophobia has become rooted and naturalized among all the peoples of the earth with whom the Jews have had relations. Judeophobia is a form of demonopathy, with the distinction that the Jewish ghost has become known to the whole race of mankind, not merely to certain races, and that it is not disembodied, like other ghosts, but is a being of flesh and blood, and suffers the most excruciating pain from the wounds inflicted upon it by the fearful mob who imagine it threatens them.

Judeophobia is a psychic aberration. As a psychic aberration, it is hereditary; as a disease transmitted for two thousand years, it is incurable.

It is the fear of ghosts, the mother of Judeophobia, which has evoked that abstract—I might call it Platonic—hatred because of which the whole Jewish nation is held responsible for the real or supposed misdeeds of its individual members, is libeled in so many ways, and is buffeted about so disgracefully.

Friend and foe alike have tried to explain or justify this hatred of the Jews by bringing all sorts of charges against them. They are said to have crucified Jesus, to have drunk the blood of Christians, to have poisoned wells, to have taken usury, to have exploited the peasant, and so on. These charges—and a thousand others of like nature—against an entire people have been proved groundless. Their falseness has been demonstrated by the very fact that they had to be trumped up wholesale in order to quiet the evil conscience of the Jew-baiters, to justify the condemnation of an entire nation, to demonstrate the necessity of burning the Jew, or rather the

Jewish ghost, at the stake. He who tries to prove too much proves nothing at all.

Though the Jews may be charged with many shortcomings, those shortcomings are, in any event, not such great vices, not such capital crimes, as to justify the condemnation of an entire people. In individual cases, indeed, we find these accusations contradicted by the fact that the Jews get along fairly well in close contact with their Gentile neighbors. This is the reason that the charges preferred are usually of the most general character, made up out of whole cloth, based to a certain degree on *a priori* reasoning, and true, at most, in individual cases, but untrue as regards the whole people.

Thus have Judaism and anti-Semitism passed for centuries through history as inseparable companions. Like the Jewish people, it seems, the real "Wandering Jew," anti-Semitism, too can never die. He must be blind indeed who will assert that the Jews are not the "chosen people," the people chosen for universal hatred. No matter how much the nations are at variance with one another, no matter how diverse in their instincts and goals, they join hands in their hatred of the Jews; on this one matter all are agreed.

The extent and manner in which this antipathy is shown depends, of course, on the cultural level of each people. The antipathy as such, however, exists in all places and at all times, no matter whether it appears in the form of violence, as envious jealousy, or under the guise of tolerance and protection. To be robbed as a Jew or to require protection as a Jew is equally humiliating, equally hurtful to the self-respect of the Jews.

Having analyzed Judeophobia as a hereditary form of demonopathy, peculiar to the human race, and having represented anti-Semitism as based on an inherited aberration of the human mind, we must draw the important conclusion: the fight against this hatred, like any fight against inherited predispositions, can only be in vain.

There were other early Zionist thinkers who approached the Jewish people's dilemma of exile, homelessness and anti-Semitism differently. One of these was Dr. Max Nordau, an early psychiatrist and one of Theodor Herzl's first supporters. Nordau eschewed the messianic yearnings of Jews that had characterized their history for long centuries. He wrote:

> The new Zionism, which has been called political, differs from the old religious, messianic variety . . . it disavows all mysticism, and does not expect the return to Palestine to be brought about by a miracle, but by its own efforts.
>
> The new Zionism has grown out of the inner impulses of Judaism itself, out of the impulses of modern, educated Jews for their history and martyrology, out of an awakened pride in their racial qualities, out of ambition to save the ancient people for a long, long future, and to add new great deeds of posterity to those of their ancestors.

HIGH POINTS IN ISRAEL'S HISTORY

In its first half-century, Israel experienced many momentous events that came to characterize the new Israeli personality as one of courage, dedication and achievement. One such event was the carefully-planned and executed kidnapping of Adolf Eichmann, the Nazi butcher responsible for the killing of untold numbers of Jews; secretly he was removed to Jerusalem, and a war crimes trial followed which eventually led to his guilty verdict and execution.

Another cathartic event was the pursuit of the Arab terrorists who murdered Israel's Olympic athletes in Munich; the terrorists were executed across the European continent.

The heroic rescue of some one hundred Jews in Uganda's Entebbe airport, despite enormous obstacles, was an event that also drew universal admiration and caused Jews worldwide to swell with pride and gratitude.

These courageous events seem to occur regularly. The transfer, by air, of over a half-million Jews from the former Soviet Union to Israel in one year was seen as such an achievement—as was the secret transfer of thousands of impoverished Ethiopian Jews to Israel in the span of two days. When Israel's largest pharmaceutical company, Teva, announced that it had developed a new medication for certain cases of multiple sclerosis, and the United States allowed it to be put on the market immediately, this was seen as a momentous accomplishment.

What originally started as a borrowed Israel air force military plane, now has become Israel's international airline, El Al (Hebrew for "to the skies"). With state of the art equipment, El Al flies westward to every major European city, continuing to New York, Newark, Washington, Miami, Chicago and Los Angeles, and extending eastward to India and other Asian

Knesset passed a new law: half of all the music heard on local radio and television must be of Israeli origin.

Concerts and musical performances are given almost nightly and in every community. When the Russian immigrants first settled in the country, they needed financial help until they found their places in Israeli society. Various groups quickly arranged performance schedules for them, in art galleries, schools, synagogues and even in private homes.

As a rule, Israelis are direct in their contact with one another. "We have no time nor patience for sham," they often explain. Generally, however, most Israelis are tactful and considerate of non-Israeli visitors, Jewish or Gentile. They have come to learn and appreciate that people from other cultures have been raised with different sets of values. They are especially eager, by and large, to speak in *dugri* terms because they live in the Middle East where tradition dictates that conversations, questions and answers should all be delivered in a roundabout way. Ironically, *dugri* is an Arabic word absorbed into Hebrew, meaning "straightforward."

Israel's radio and television channels close down for the Sabbath and Jewish religious holidays, with some exceptions. People in the country who are unable to get along without them, can easily tune into American, British and European stations, as well as to those in nearby Arab lands. Every hour in Israel, the news comes on; if one is in a taxi or a bus, the driver often raises the volume automatically so that everyone can hear.

Almost every home in Israel owns a television set. Minorities can listen to television and radio programs from Egypt, Syria, Lebanon and Jordan. It always amuses visitors to the southern Negev region to see television antennas affixed to the uppermost poles of Bedouin tents.

CULINARY TRADITIONS

Although it is fair to say that in the early years Israel's culinary traditions left a great deal to be desired, that has completely changed now. Major hotels employ European-trained chefs who have succeeded in elevating the country's culinary quality enormously. There are wholesome restaurants throughout Israel, offering Chinese, Thai, Indian, Middle Eastern, East European, and Western-style cuisine.

All public establishments—the armed forces, government offices, hotels, schools—maintain kosher dining rooms. Non-kosher restaurants are also available. Many dishes feature the standard Mediterranean hummus. Although Israelis are not known to be heavy drinkers, and Moslems are forbidden to consume any alcohol, a fine array of wines and liquors is always available. Of course, at the very least, Jewish families usually drink a little wine at the weekly Sabbath eve family dinner. Many wines and liquors are exported around the world. Oddly, soon after the former Soviet regime collapsed, there was a shortage of vodka, a staple for many East Europeans; and one of the countries that shipped vodka to Moscow was Israel.

There are modern, efficient supermarkets throughout the country as well as small, "mom-and-pop" grocery shops. The Sabbath bread, called *chalah*, is packed into nearly everyone's shopping cart on Friday afternoon. It is a soft, white bread used to bless the arrival of the weekly Sabbath.

GETTING AROUND IN ISRAEL

Israel has a convenient bus system which connects every corner of the country. Usually modern and comfortable, buses take passengers, at low fares, from the major cities to every point in Israel. Although there are, of course, numerous private cars on the road, it is generally agreed that there are not enough roads. All major highways provide clear directions in English as well as in Hebrew and Arabic, and could easily be mistaken for the best and newest of American parkways.

There are also taxis which by law must operate on meters, although some drivers work out flat rates, especially for long trips. There are small planes connecting Tel Aviv and Eilat, as well as Haifa and a few small civilian airports. A pleasant, scenic journey is available on the railroad between Tel Aviv and Haifa; a long but spectacular scenic train ride is offered between Jerusalem and Tel Aviv.

A phenomenon to people from western countries is the sight of young Israelis floating in the air above Israel's coastal areas on the Sabbath. They are relaxing on the traditional day of rest in a most unusual manner: their arms stretched out, colorful parachutes strapped to their backs, soaring over the coasts with enviable ease.

Transportation to Israel has evolved into a jet-age routine; planes from New York make the non-stop trip in about ten hours. Many European airlines fly in from their home bases, usually in a matter of hours. Tourist ships also call at the ports of Haifa and Ashdod on the Mediterranean. Occasionally, Eilat, the southernmost port on the Gulf of Aqaba leading to the Red Sea, will welcome a private yacht. Primarily, Eilat is a busy import and export port, connecting Israel to Asia and eastern Africa via the Indian Ocean.

POLITICS AND GOVERNMENT

While Israel is a full-fledged democracy—often said to be the only genuine democracy in the Middle East—its politics and governmental traditions can be difficult to absorb for foreigners, especially Americans. The top official approved by the Knesset is the president. He has little real power: he can order the release of prisoners or have their sentences reduced, and he can appoint judges.

The prime minister, who is now chosen directly by the electorate, is the most powerful individual in the country; in the past he had generally been selected by the leading political party in the Knesset.

In Israel's early years all prime ministers—called *rosh hamemshala*—were leaders of the centrist Labor party; in more recent years there have also been *Likud* (a conservative party) prime ministers. The prime minister chooses his own cabinet members, but they must be approved by the Knesset. The 120-member Knesset is Israel's national legislative body, which has always included Arab and Druze members.

Both during the Labor and Likud administrations, the government was compelled to include coalition members of small parties; these generally joined the government on the condition that their interests and demands be met. For legislation to be approved in the Knesset, a vote of at least sixty-one—a simple majority—is required. Neither Labor nor Likud administration has ever had sixty-one of its people elected to the Knesset. Hence, coalitions have always been necessary.

The judiciary is fiercely independent, although legally it reports to the prime minister. The chief of staff of the armed forces and of the police, the attorney-general, and the governor of the Bank of Israel are all appointed by the prime minister, with cabinet approval. Some of the president's official duties are ceremonial, such as receiving and accepting newly-named diplomatic envoys to Israel.

Local officials—mayors and municipal councils—are elected on a local basis. Governing Israel requires, inter alia, great skills because of the plethora of small parties, each seeking to gain advantages for its own programs. This usually comes down to funds for schools, social welfare programs, and influence in the community through control of certain government offices.

Because of "coalition politics" and the contradictory demands of many small parties, election campaigns often become heated affairs. By law the national elections are held every four years. However, if a vote of no confidence in the sitting prime minister passes, new elections take place soon after such a vote.

Israel's presidents in the past have included chemists (Chaim Weizmann, Ephraim Katzir), scholars (Yitzhak Ben Zvi, Zalman Shazar), and retired generals (Chaim Herzog, Ezer Weizman). Prime ministers have included political leaders (David Ben Gurion, Golda Meir), generals (Yitzhak Rabin, Ehud Barak), and one lawyer (Menahem Begin).

EVERY SIXTH ISRAELI

Of every six Israeli citizens, one belongs to a minority group. These include over seventy-six percent Moslems, over thirteen percent Christians, over seven percent Druze, and three far smaller groups: Karaites, Samaritans and Circassians. The Moslem total includes a large sub-group of Bedouins; the Karaites and Samaritans have historic links to centuries-old Jewish roots.

Many, and perhaps most, younger generation Moslems are almost indistinguishable from Jewish Israelis. Most of Israel's Moslems belong to the Sunni branch; usually Sunnis are less rigid in their religious observance than the Shi'ites. Some Israeli Moslems attend the Hebrew University in Jerusalem; many also enroll in Haifa University. In the past some have chosen to study at the Arab University of Bir Zeit, in the West Bank.

Most of the country's Bedouin population resides in the northern Negev area; however, growing numbers have opted to move to towns where their children can receive a higher education.

The Circassians, numbering nearly four thousand, are Moslems of European origin who migrated to Palestine from Ukraine in the 1880s. Many have blond hair and blue eyes. They have always served in the Israeli armed forces.

Christians in Israel usually are Greek Catholics; there are also Greek Orthodox and Maronites. Mostly they conduct services in Arabic. The Druze are members of a secret religion, which is said to be a breakaway from the mainstream Moslem faith. The Druze in Israel serve in the armed forces with distinction, and have always maintained a strong friendship with the Jewish majority. Mostly they reside in the Carmel mountain range.

The Karaites, who number some 15,000 and who originate in the Crimea area, are recognized by the Israeli rabbis as Jews, despite the fact that they do not accept the Oral Law, i.e., the teachings and laws of the Talmud. Marriage between Jews and Karaites is permitted despite the latter's nonconformist views.

The Karaite, Shulamit Aloni, a women's rights activist, has been a Knesset member.

Samaritans claim descent from the Ten Lost Tribes. They deny that they are Jews, even though their traditions and customs closely resemble Judaic teachings. They number only several hundred and live both in Holon, a Tel Aviv suburb, and near Nablus, on Mount Gerizim in the West Bank which they deem sacred. There is virtually no marriage between them and Israeli Jews.

Although members of the Bahai faith are very few in Israel, they maintain their holy shrine in Haifa and consider this location the religious focus of their worldwide faith. Their shrine features a golden-domed temple, much like the better-known Mosque of Omar in Jerusalem.

ECONOMIC DEVELOPMENT

The pioneering economy that the first Jewish settlers in Palestine developed centered on citriculture. Later the settlers grew vineyards, and over time expanded their collective and cooperative farms to include a much wider variety of crops.

Industrial and various other commercial enterprises came later. By the 1970s, Israel was assured that its economy would in time enable the country to feed itself, provide for all its people's needs, and even earn foreign currency through exports. Utilizing the most scientific know-how, Israel learned how to grow more crops on less land, and how to make those food products available overseas.

American and European supermarket customers, in the middle of winter, may find it astounding to see Israeli fresh-grown tomatoes for sale; this is also amazing to Israelis. Gradually, agronomists and other farming experts realized that the vast Negev desert, which remains warm and summer-like throughout the winter months, could be coaxed to grow what are usually considered warm-weather fruits and vegetables.

In addition to food products exported from Israel, notably in the winter months, a veritable flower industry has flourished in the country year-round. In the dead of winter, particularly in England, France and Germany, flower lovers can obtain their favorite floral wreaths, courtesy of Israel's year-long growing season, much of it focused in the southern Negev.

In the 1980s, soon after the Information Age took over one industrial economy after another, Israelis realized that this brand-new scientific discipline was what they had been looking for. Software offerings began to be created by tiny Israeli companies, often launched in someone's garage. The response was immediate and electric. Computer-linked products did not require vast outlays of money or huge amounts of plant space; and within a few short years, Israel began to be recognized worldwide as one of the most advanced and successful suppliers of hardware and software.

Earlier, Israeli companies had made great strides in medical technology, creating ultra-sophisticated scanning devices for hospitals around the world. In the 1990s the arrival of highly-educated Jewish engineers and scientists from the former Soviet Union has spurred this expansion of Israel's new information and medical technology even further. This growth has led some agricultural collectives to sell their valuable land in exchange for continued industrial expansion.

HOLIDAYS AND SYMBOLS

Although all of its citizens have equal rights, Israel regards itself as Jewish, the only such state in the world. Therefore, when Jewish holidays and festivals come around, the whole country seems to take part. At the very least, everyone is excused from work and school. Israel also has its own Jewish calendar, which is lunar, although the global Gregorian calendar is widely-used.

The work week in Israel starts Sunday morning and ends, generally, on Friday afternoon. In recent years more and more Israelis have been working a five-day week, Sunday through Thursday. All holidays (which are religious in nature) and festivals (which are not), like the weekly Sabbath, begin the prior evening. The Jewish lunar calendar also has its own names for the months of the year.

In February or March (Hebrew month *Shvat*), Israelis mark the festival of Tu B'shvat, the New Year for Trees; in February or March *(Adar)*, the festival of Purim recounts Queen Esther's rescue of threatened Jews; in March or April *(Nissan)*, Passover holiday recalls the ancient exodus of Israelite slaves from Egypt; May *(Iyar)* marks the Israel Independence Day festival; in June *(Sivan)*, S'havuot celebrates the First Fruits harvest, which recalls the tradition when God gave the Torah to Moses; in July or August *(Av)*, the sad fast day of Tisha B'av occurs, marking the destruction of the Holy Temples in Jerusalem; in September *(Tishrai)* the High Holy Days of Rosh Hashanah and Yom Kippur take place, followed by the Sukkot holiday and the joyous Simchat Torah celebration. These latter holidays usually extend into October. November *(Heshvan)* has no celebrations, but December *(Kislev)* marks the popular Hanukkah festival.

Americans residing or visiting in Israel are often surprised to find that Thanksgiving Day is commemorated, at least by the consumption of a traditional turkey meal.

During Tu B'shvat, thousands plant tree saplings; on Purim, there are masquerade parties; Passover traditionally is a family holiday when, in lieu of bread, matza is eaten for a week recalling the Israelites hasty departure from Egypt; on Shavuot, worshipers on their way to synagogue may be seen carrying palm branches; on Tisha B'av, synagogues hold mournful worship services; Rosh Hashanah and Yom Kippur, known as the Days of Awe, is a time for extending holiday good wishes to friends and family; on Sukkot, Israelis put hut-like structures on their balconies or lawns; on Simchat Torah, there is exuberant rejoicing and the carrying of the Scrolls of the Law through the streets; during Hanukkah, candles are lit every evening to recall the miracle of the Temple rededication by the Maccabees.

It is a Sephardic festival custom for many public institutions to hand out jelly donuts (*sufganiyot*) to one and all during Hanukkah. The donuts, heavy with oil, recall the festival's miracle, when a cruse of oil lasted for eight days. Since many non-Jewish tourists visit Israel during the Christmas holidays, the larger hotels in recent years have begun to have a Santa Claus on the premises, to make the visitors feel more at home.

ISRAEL AT LEISURE

Typically, Israelis are hard-working, and thus regard leisure— true rest—as a valuable commodity. As early as nursery school, young Israelis are taught to exercise regularly. It is not unusual to see Israelis on the beach, both in winter and summer, doing strenuous exercises.

Every four years since 1932 there has been a Maccabiah, a kind of Jewish Olympics, held in Israel. Athletes from all parts of the world compete in weight-lifting, soccer, track and wrestling. Two very popular sports in Israel are basketball and tennis, in addition to the old standby, soccer. Efforts have been made to introduce baseball into the country, but it has met with only limited success. One eighteen-hole golf course in Caeserea exists for avid golfers. There is also a racing track for automobiles.

Most Israelis enjoy swimming, in pools as well as along the coast of the Mediterranean. Many are also ardent picnickers and enthusiastic hikers. They explain that this is not only good exercise, but an enjoyable way to rediscover their ancient land. The Israel Defense Force has developed a series of challenging exercises designed to make every soldier as self-reliant as possible; one in particular consists of hiking through difficult terrain, carrying a heavy backpack.

Behind Israel's leaders' planning for the future is the never-to-be-forgotten tragedy of the Holocaust. Israel seeks to build unto perpetuity a democracy that is strong—one which will embrace the biblical teachings of morality and justice, and attract an ever-larger Jewish population.

Perhaps that is why Israeli recruits, when sworn in either at the Western Wall in Jerusalem or atop Masada, the ancient site of Jewish resistance to Roman oppression, are handed two items: a rifle and a Bible.

Often described as a land of sharp contrasts, Israel has a modern, eighteen-hole golf course in Caeserea in the north, where relics of the Roman era are commonplace.

A LOOK AT THE FUTURE

Although the universal and eternal prophets of the Hebrew Bible have made Israel's name almost synonymous with prophecy, Jewish tradition states clearly that the prophetic age has come and gone.

Looking into the future is therefore an activity not recommended for logical, rational people. That having been said, it nonetheless is something that has to be done.

Why? For the simple reason that although the course of Jewish history has never run smoothly for very long, somehow there has always been a sense that gradually, slowly, but unquestionably, things will get better.

To put it another way, Jews have sensed that the people of Israel, and now the State of Israel, have a mission that is never-ending and certainly far from complete: the tradition of *tikun olam.* Literally translated this means "fixing the world"; actually, this phrase suggests that one should strive to be "God's partner" in improving world conditions, thus making it a healthier and more positive world for all people.

The Bible's emphasis on pursuing justice and morality essentially focuses on the same goal. For people in the modern State of Israel, looking for a good life for themselves and their children is the utmost priority—just like people of all faiths and backgrounds around the world.

However, difficult as it is to express, the people of Israel also sense that they have an additional, special mission. Establishing the State of Israel on its ancestral soil after nearly two millennia of exile, only three years after the defeat of Nazism which succeeded in wiping out one-third of the world's Jewish population, and creating in some fifty years a modern, upbeat, democratic country whose Jewish population is approaching five million—all this has produced among Israelis and Jews abroad a sense of awe.

Even among the most irreligious Jews in Israel and in all parts of the world, there is a mystical feeling that everything— the Holocaust, Israel's creation and defeat of far larger and stronger Arab armies, Israel's ascendancy in the worlds of science and medicine—has been divinely pre-ordained.

Of course there will be pessimists who will see things otherwise and question: What of the conflicts between the ultra-Orthodox and totally secular? And between Jews and Arabs, both inside and outside Israel? And what about conflicts with neighboring states?

To which there is one answer. During the past one hundred years, prior to the establishment of Israel and since then, one answer has been given in Hebrew to worriers, pessimists and nay-sayers who are skeptical of a glorious future: *yi'hi'ye tov.* "It will be okay."

INDEX